A LIFE OF GIVING

Published in 2016 by Glengarden Press
Ballater, Aberdeenshire, Scotland

British Library Cataloguing in Publication Data

A catalogue record for this book is available from the British Library

ISBN 978-0-9547552-7-0

Layout by Catherine Hollingworth

Printed by McKenzie Print Ltd, Aberdeen

Copies of this book are available from:
Rhod McEwan at
Glengarden Press
Ballater, Aberdeenshire
AB35 5UB Scotland
Tel: (013397) 55429
email: teeoff@rhodmcewan.com

A LIFE OF
GIVING

Sheila Ferres
with Jo Booth

Sheila E. Ferres.

Glengarden Press
Ballater Aberdeenshire

With thanks to:

George Booth
Mike Fielder
Mary Greig
Feona McEwan
Rhod McEwan
Agnes McKenzie
Heather Morrison
Sue Sexton Reid
Jean Wood

All proceeds from the sale of this book will be donated to CHART. If you would like to make a donation to CHART, please send to:

Sheila Ferres
Greenferns
Watson Street
BANCHORY
AB31 5UB

Chapter One

'Tell me, what have you done for someone else today?'

This was the question asked by Sheila Ferres's parents, every day, of both herself and her two sisters which they in turn would answer with an explanation of whom they had helped with simple acts of kindness and caring. It is this philosophy of giving to others which Sheila has practised since, and it is this generosity of spirit which she credits for her long, happy and fulfilling life. Her career as a physiotherapist has spanned more than seventy years, and she is the oldest registered and practising physiotherapist in the UK, still seeing patients and consulting with other medical professionals. She combines this with her relatively new career as a successful watercolourist, which she began fifteen years ago.

Sheila Ferres, née Bennett, was born in the village of Heaton, West Yorkshire, on the 3rd May 1923 to Stephen and Elsie Bennett, the third daughter following her sisters Patricia and Ailsa. The three girls were very close in age, all born within four years of each other. Sheila remembers her childhood with great fondness:

> 'My upbringing was entirely blessed in every way. We were extremely fortunate not just in our material circumstances, but also in our wonderful and gifted parents.'

Sheila's family prosperity initially came from her great grandfather, John Bennett who founded the Bennett Steamship Company. In 1876, John Bennett established a weekly steamship crossing between Goole – which is located up the Humber River past Hull – and Calais, but within a year he had altered the destination to the more profitable Boulogne and started running two crossings a week. To begin with John Bennett concentrated on cargoes of fruit and flowers, but over the life of the company they adapted to carrying other cargoes, such as coal or cars. The company was originally known as 'The Red Cross Line Company' and its ensign was a white flag with a blue outer border and a central red cross. It also established a tradition of naming all their steamships with titles ending in 'a' – their first ship was called 'Hydra', followed later by 13 further ships with names such as Syria, Corea, Sparta, and Africa. This became a family tradition echoed in the names chosen by Sheila's parents for their own daughters, namely Patricia, Ailsa and Sheila.

The Bennett Steamships were naturally requisitioned to help with the war effort in both the First and Second World Wars, and suffered huge losses at sea. Sheila can remember listening to the radio with her parents when it was announced that the last of the family liners had been lost, with a huge loss of life. Eventually what was left of the company was sold in 1948, when Sheila was twenty five, to the General Steam Company, which later became part of P&O Shipping. There is still a plaque to the Bennett family on the wall in Boulogne Harbour.

The original John Bennett had two sons amongst his many children, named John, born 1862, and Robert, born 1865 and the family lived in a large house in Goole named Grove House. Sheila reminisces:

'I remember as a child going to Grove House and picking walnuts off the trees in the garden – it was quite idyllic.'

There were many stories of the family passed down to Sheila, including one of her grandfather Robert Bennett, who being the son of one of the wealthiest and successful businessmen of the area, became the victim of a kidnap plot in 1868:

'Robert was a very fair child, almost albino in his colouring, quite distinctive. Years before, when Robert was only three, he was kidnapped. A lady who happened to be in Goole at the time saw a Gypsy caravan going along the road and

saw the curtain being drawn back by a very small child
with extremely fair hair. This was my grandfather, and
when it was announced in the papers that he had been
kidnapped, this woman was able to tell the police what
she had seen, and he was rescued unharmed.'

As might have been expected, as the brothers grew to adulthood,
they became very interested in the family business and were keen to
help their father John to develop it. The younger John remained in
Goole, whilst Robert went to Boulogne. The company was at its most
successful around this time, late nineteenth century, and was now
conveying fruit, flowers and vegetables to the markets at Convent
Garden from Boulogne via Goole. John married an English lady, and
they had two children, one of whom was a daughter named Elsie
Bennett, born 1892. Robert settled in Boulogne, married a French
lady and went on to have five children among them a son named
Stephen Bennett, born in 1889. As Sheila explains:

'The children travelled backwards and forwards on the
boats in their school holidays and the cousins became
great friends. Stephen was eventually naturalised as
a British citizen and joined the British army, and after a
while he and Elsie became very close and were married.
These two were my parents. We are, therefore the result
of two cousins marrying. My maiden name was Bennett,
as was my mother's, of course. The two brothers, John
and Robert, were my grandfathers.'

Sheila remembers her paternal grandmother, Robert's wife, received
the highest award for bravery in France for a tremendous act of
courage, which happened just before the outbreak of World War Two.

'One night there was a huge storm and a boat was sinking
in the harbour at Boulogne. All the passengers were thrown
into the water. My grandmother dived off Boulogne pier,
even as the storm was still raging, and rescued as many
of them as she was able, bringing them out to the water's
edge. I think, actually, it was the height of the harbour

that was the truly extraordinary thing as the dockside was extremely high and the tide exceptionally low, and therefore the performance of such a feat would have required breath-taking courage.'

Sheila was only eight when her maternal grandmother, John's wife, died. Many of her aunts and uncles moved abroad to different countries all over the world, but one of her father's sisters, Queenie, remained in France and spent many holidays with a very young Sheila and her family. Sheila had one uncle on her mother's side named William Bennett, known as 'Billy', who was a very clever and successful engineer, working for the British Thomson-Houston Company in Rugby. He signed up during the First World War and in 1917 he was posted to Russia to assemble and test British planes for the Russians and also to train their air force personnel. Sheila takes up the story:

'My uncle, Captain William Bennett, was captured and taken prisoner, but he escaped with a friend who was also his commanding officer, Major James Valentine, and they spent a week or so on motorbikes getting away back to their units. Although Major Valentine was later to die in Russia, Billy eventually arrived back in this country and was awarded the Military Cross. There is a record of what he did in the RAF Museum along with his medal which was donated by his wife. Billy and his wife had only one child who sadly died after contracting measles, and then Billy died at the young age of thirty eight of pneumonia. So that terminated the Bennett family on that side.'

Sheila has always maintained that her life has always been full of the most fortuitous coincidences.

'Many uncanny, extraordinarily lucky connections have happened to me. I think everything is somehow connected. There isn't one thing you can suggest that doesn't lead you to something else. That's how it seems to me anyway.'

Recently, at a meeting concerning one of the charities Sheila works closely with, a gentleman whom she did not know took the seat next to her:

'He didn't have a local accent so I asked him where he was from. 'You won't know it,' he said. 'It's a place called Goole.' I laughed and said 'I certainly know Goole. Does the Bennett Steamship Company mean anything to you?' 'Of course' he replied. So I said, 'I am the last survivor of the Bennett Steamship Company.' 'I can't believe it!' he said and appeared totally amazed. 'I run Goole museum. We've got models of your liners. We've got information all around the museum of the Bennett Steamship Company and there is even a book published of its history. This is absolutely unreal.'

When he was home a week or two later, he sent me recent photographs of Grove House, photographs of the museum, the harbour, every mortal thing. There was also an artist by the name of Reuben Chappell who painted some of the earlier ships, examples of which can be seen in the Goole Museum and Art Gallery.'

Chapter Two

Both of Sheila's parents were very good at sports, her mother was an accomplished hockey player and her father a talented golfer, and they encouraged a love of sports in Sheila and her sisters. They played many games as a family, a favourite of which was Croquet. Sheila was by far the most active of the sisters, even alone she would spend many hours on her trapeze swing in the garden hanging upside down, doing gymnastics and wonders today if she might have been a 'hyperactive' child if that label had existed then. At the time of Sheila's birth her parents engaged the services of a resident Nanny, Elsie Coates, who would become very dear to the family, and who also shared their belief that the girls needed regular exercise, especially 'lively little Sheila'. Consequently from a very young age, Sheila can remember walking for miles in the afternoons around the local countryside in the company of her sisters and Nanny, and playing many outdoor games.

'Naturally there were lots of places to roam. I particularly remember Nanny taking us fairly frequently to Ilkley Moor, which was a great day's outing, especially to the Cow and Calf rocks. Nanny taught us so many things, and I suppose I must have been naughty at some point, as all children are, but I don't remember. It was Nanny's job to control my extremely active nature. She had been in our wider family for many years and she came to us when I was born. She stayed with us for fourteen years, long after we had realistically needed a nanny, but because she was so dear to us. She eventually left to go to another family just a few doors away to help a handicapped child, but unfortunately died just a few years later from a brain tumour.'

This love of being active dominated Sheila's childhood and she wryly remembers that:

'I believe, in fact, that the parents of some childhood friends of mine used to find it a rather horrible thought that I was coming to stay for the weekend because they knew that everyone was likely to be kept active from morning to night!'

As a keen sportsman himself, Sheila's father would spend many hours with Sheila playing a game they called 'Come Back'. Sheila explains:

'It consisted of a supporting frame with a tennis ball hung from it on the end of a piece of elastic. In those days, eighty four years ago, we must have had one of the first ones, but they became very popular in the sixties. They wrecked the grass of course, but I used to stand in the garden for hours playing that.'

This early version of 'Swingball' was the first taste Sheila had of tennis, a sport which was to become of huge importance to her, often playing a major part in influencing her decisions on the direction her life would take. Elsie, Sheila's mother, was also blessed of an enquiring mind and taught her daughters all about their local countryside, the names of the wildflowers, which they would gather and press to keep in books, and also the birds and wildlife. She was in addition a tremendously gifted seamstress, making all her daughters' clothes, beautifully hand smocking their dresses, all the curtains and other household furnishings, and even upholstering furniture. Sheila explains how her mother passed these gifts on to her:

'Eventually I made all my clothes, blouses and so forth, everything my mother did. My sisters did not; they weren't interested. They couldn't even knit. I did absolutely everything and anything there was to do, then and always have done'.

Throughout her life Sheila not only made clothing for herself, her sisters and later, her husband but has also put these skills to good use in aid of many charities. When Sheila was five, she followed her sisters to school at Rossfield Primary:

'This wonderful, local private school furthered me in my active life and my interest in everything, by giving us each a plot of garden within the school grounds which we had to look after. The school also took us on rambling walks every single week into the country, so between home and school, I was well versed in all things in nature. The total effect was the finest basis for a person's life to have a broad field. Later we were to be sent to different secondary schools as we all got older, but we all went to Rossfield Preparatory School until we were eleven or twelve.

I suppose people would say that we lived spoilt lives, but my mother made sure that despite all the advantages of our privileged upbringing, we were taught how important it was to help others wherever we could. Every single day, in the late afternoon, my mother would ask us what we had done for someone else that day. We were taught the importance of that from very early on, and that has always been a major part of my life, doing things for everybody else and remains so. It was a wonderful thing to teach your children and I do thank my mother greatly for passing it on to me.

I remember a childhood incident with my eldest sister, Pat. We'd all just been given our pocket money to spend as we wished in a little sweet shop in the village, one of the treats of our week. We crossed the road and there we saw a tramp, who obviously had very little, and was trudging along and trudging along. Pat went up to him and said, 'I've just been given my pocket money. I would like to give it to you because you look as if you could do with it more than me.' He looked at her in surprise

and said, 'You're one of the kindest lassies I've ever met.'
So she gave it to him. It was a very natural thing for her
to do – perfectly normal.

As a result of my mother's teachings, I've spent the
whole of my seventy five adult years trying my best to do
things for other people, never considering anything else
other than helping everybody else, both with my career
and in every other part of my life. We were taught to
appreciate every single thing we had and be grateful for
it, and to be grateful to anyone who ever did anything
for us. We were told that just because we had virtually
everything they could give us, we were not going to be
spoilt. We were definitely going to do everything for
everybody else.'

Another important part of the girls' upbringing involved the
development and training of their memories, something that again
Sheila credits with helping her to maintain her mental health and
agility as she has got older. She believes that the same emphasis
placed upon keeping the body fit and agile should also be given to
exercising the mind.

As well as reporting back on their daily good deed, in the
evening time the girls were given a list of things to remember, which
they were to relate at the following morning's breakfast.

'I think one of the finest things you can do when you are
young, is to develop your memory. As a student later on,
I found it tremendously helpful because I would compose
a list of things I needed to recall, and then leave it on the
dressing table. In the morning I would read it, and then
I would have to recall it again in the evening. I have done
this the whole of my life so that even at the age of ninety
two, now, I can recall more telephone numbers than anyone
else I know. I don't have to look them up; car numbers as
well. So I've got a very retentive mind.'

This 'training' of her memory was to serve Sheila very well throughout
her life but never more so than when she was studying later on.

Sheila and her sisters spent the majority of their time with Nanny as was common at that time, whilst her father ran his business and her mother oversaw the running of the household, with the services of a resident cook and maid. Sheila's father was in a partnership and owned a large emporium in Bradford dealing in art and needlework supplies, the only other similar establishment at the time existed in Regent Street in London. They sold needlework, wool, tapestries, and anything else to support all the hobbies that were popular at the time. Sheila can remember the excitement of him visiting France, to bring back such luxuries as angora wool. Unfortunately at the height of this success, the partner died prematurely and as there was a shortfall in the insurance payout, Sheila's father had to buy out the Partner's share. After that Mr Bennett ran a smaller concern on his own until the business was sold at the end of the forties, and the premises bought by F.W. Woolworth and Co Ltd.

Sheila often speaks of her childhood and has always thought she was very privileged not only in a materialistic sense but also in the inspiring people she had around her:

'To me, the whole basis of my life has been my parents and the influence they had on me as a child. Thanks to their efforts and those of our Nanny, also a wonderful woman, I feel I had a very interesting childhood.

Mother was a pianist; her father had given her a grand piano for her twenty first birthday. Father had a very lovely singing voice, and every Sunday we would all gather in the drawing room where Mother would play for us, and Father would sing to encourage a love of classical music which remains with me to this day. Father was also in the amateur dramatic society so he was hugely entertaining, always making us laugh. I think my favourite childhood memories are of those Sunday afternoons, of the music and the fun, and of the family all being together.'

Chapter 3

Elsie and Stephen Bennett were concerned that as their three girls were so close in age, they may overtake one another academically, and that this in turn may cause rivalry amongst them or perhaps cause one or other to lose confidence. Consequently after much thought and deliberation, they originally decided to send each of the girls to a different school, yet circumstances were to conspire against this decision. Pat, the eldest, was sent to Harrogate Ladies College, a prestigious girls' boarding school but within months, she contracted Scarlet Fever which, before the advent of antibiotics, was a serious childhood disease. Pat returned home to recover but shortly after, Ailsa and Sheila also developed the symptoms and were themselves confined to bed in isolation at home for six weeks, the standard procedure at the time. Sheila remembers this as a particularly frustrating and testing time for a child who was used to being very active:

> 'Initially I was too ill and weak to care much about
> anything. I remember getting out of bed, my legs giving
> way beneath me and just collapsing to the floor. I had never
> experienced anything like it before. Gradually we began
> to recover, and I found this period of recovery particularly
> difficult as I was used to being so active. Nanny was still
> with us, of course, and so she was coming and going, to and
> from the bedroom, but otherwise we were allowed very few
> visitors, and one had to entertain oneself the whole time.
> I can remember sleeping for a considerable amount of time,
> but I can also remember being very bored and frustrated.

One of the only other people allowed to visit us was my Godmother who lived in the village, and I have vivid memories of her arriving on a regular basis, and sitting and chatting to us. She used to bring the most beautiful chocolate biscuits you ever saw, wrapped in silver, red and green paper – a real treat for the invalids! Eventually, as I improved, I used to get up and go for little walking spells to the garden and back again – thankful that I was at last allowed outside in the fresh air again.'

For Pat, Harrogate College had not been a happy experience. Previously, before succumbing to Scarlet Fever, she had also been badly injured when taking part in a fire alarm exercise, which involved her jumping into an enclosed escape chute from an above ground window. Consequently, when she was fully recovered from Scarlet Fever, it was decided that she would resume her education at an alternative boarding school, Lowther College, in Wales. Mr and Mrs Bennett had chosen Lowther largely because it offered a wide range of extracurricular activities and sports, including its own golf course and they continued to believe in the importance of their daughters remaining physically active. When she was of age, Ailsa joined Pat at Lowther, but as Pat continued to enjoy playing sports, and other activities such as hill climbing and walking, Ailsa had, within two years, developed pneumonia so severely that she was unexpected to live. Ailsa returned home and with careful nursing and constant rest over a significant period of time, she did recover, but her heart had been irrevocably damaged, and remained weak for the rest of her life. Ailsa thus lived a sedentary life, unable to cope with any strenuous exercise, but she compensated by developing an extensive knowledge and interest of English Literature. As Sheila observes:

'Ailsa had a totally different life to Patricia and myself, as we remained constantly physically active, playing different sports, walking, climbing and so on, but poor Ailsa was forced to lead a very quiet life from aged fourteen onwards. In those days, if you got an infection, one of the first procedures was to take all your teeth out, a completely outdated notion these days. The doctors believed that

somehow Alisa's teeth must have contributed to the
infection in some way so they removed all her teeth, which
must have been horrible for a young girl. It seems absurd
now, but that was the thinking in the 1930's. Thankfully,
none of this would take place nowadays, due to the advent
of antibiotics.'

During this time, Sheila, as the youngest, remained at Rossfield Prep
School where she continued to develop her love of sport, and in
particular tennis. Although Sheila was later to emulate her mother's
talent for hockey and go on to represent her county, it would be
her passion and talent for tennis, which would guide not only her
educational choices but also the direction of her later career.

Sheila's parents recognized that their youngest daughter not
only showed enormous enthusiasm for playing tennis but also a
prodigious talent as well. Sheila attributes this in part to the fact that
her arms were 5 inches longer than average which combined with
her adult height of 5ft. 11ins made her a formidable opponent. In
Heaton, there was, coincidentally, one of the foremost tennis clubs in
the country. The excellence of the facilities, including the provision
of at least twelve courts attracted many contestants, some of whom
were ex-Wimbledon players, which in turn led to an extraordinarily
high standard of play. Consequently it was decided that when Sheila
left Rossfield, she would remain at home and attend Bradford Girls
Grammar School, in order to be given the best opportunity to develop
her tennis. Sheila explains:

'My parents decided it would be better if I remained
at a local school so I could get tennis coaching, and be
able to play matches at the weekends and so forth. Ailsa
joined me at this local school for the last two years of her
education until she had matriculated, because she was too
unwell to return to boarding school. Luckily we had some
local family friends who owned their own tennis court.
They used to invite me round a lot so I could practise
and we also had tennis parties, so I would be there most
weekends. Everything in my life at that stage seemed to
involve tennis in some way. This included my social life

too, as all my friends were tennis enthusiasts. Playing at
the Heaton Tennis Club was always a delightful challenge
because of the high standard of play, which of course is
the best way to learn. It was always doubles at that time,
and as there was a large membership, we kept on changing
partners and so forth, so there were endless opportunities
to play. I also had tennis coaching both at the school and
the Club, but then, in 1939, when I was sixteen, the war
started and all that came to a grinding halt.'

Heaton was only a small country village at the time of the war, so
it was not a target for the German Air Force. However Sheila and
her family often heard the bombs dropping on the industrial areas
of Leeds and Bradford, and could see the skies lit up by the burning
cities. There were many times when the air raid sirens would go off,
and they would all gather in the basement of their house, thankful
for the protection it offered them.

Sheila left school in 1940, at the age of 17 with her matriculation.
Instead of the modern system of a separate qualification for each
subject, at that time pupils chose their subjects, and upon passing
their exams they would achieve either a school certificate or if they
passed at a higher grade they would receive their matriculation.
Sheila explains her choices of subject as thus:

'Obviously I studied maths, no doubt influenced by my
winning the Headmaster's maths prize in primary school.
I studied all the sciences, biology, chemistry and physics,
and due to my enjoyment of the countryside, botany. You
had to do English and French also but I didn't enjoy history
or geography.'

Mr and Mrs Bennett had always made it clear to their daughters that
they expected each of them to have a career, an unusually progressive
attitude before the war. However as World War Two approached, the
huge social upheaval led to a great many women taking on the jobs
that had previously been held by the thousands of men conscripted
to the Armed Forces. Many people from different social classes, who
had never been in paid employment, found themselves conscripted to

the workplace, and of course none more so than health professionals such as doctors, nurses, and all the associate services. When Ailsa was nineteen, she was accepted at the prestigious Guy's Hospital in London to begin her training as a nurse. This was at the very beginning of the war, and to avoid the bombing in London, Guys relocated many of their students to other hospitals in safer locations to continue their training. As Sheila goes on to explain:

'Ailsa started her training in Orpington, Kent, where she was living with a family whose own daughter was training to be a physiotherapist, and Ailsa thought that I might like that too. She wrote to me and said 'This girl is definitely living the sort of life that you would like. Think about it and consider whether you would like physiotherapy as a career.'

Of course it wasn't called 'Physiotherapy' until 1944, and was referred to as 'Massage and Medical Gymnastics' before then, when as practitioners we were called masseurs and masseuses. Naturally it was a reserved occupation during wartime. Obviously I did think about it and realized that it was, absolutely the most perfect career for someone of my nature. It involved a great deal of physical activity and a deep understanding of the human body, which for me, as a sportswoman, was ideal. I was fully aware of the way in which the human body works and its capability, which has proved pivotal to my work. My love of sport and my love of physiotherapy were to become inextricably entwined, just as I suspected the minute Ailsa made the suggestion. Therefore I put in my application and was accepted to start my training with Guy's at Orpington with Ailsa. It was the beginning of a career, which would span over seventy years and which has been the whole focus of my life, and the expression of all those values I learnt as a child – to help other people and indeed, to always be looking for new ways to help others. What a very lucky person I am.'

Chapter 4

When Sheila started her training at the Guy's Hospital in Orpington, Ailsa had already completed three years of her nursing training. Although there was three years between them, they were very physically alike, and often mistaken for one another, sometimes using this to their advantage.

Ailsa now lived in the nurses' home and was entitled to eat in the hospital canteen, but Sheila was in digs, and along with many colleagues, struggled to survive on her meagre rations and maintains that she 'spent the entire war lying awake at night wondering how and where to get something to eat'. Sheila's solution to her predicament was to make use of her similarity to Ailsa and explains:

> 'One day I said to Ailsa 'Do you mind if I borrow your uniform and go into the canteen in the nurses' home? Can you also tell me where you normally sit? I must eat a meal.' I went into the dining room wearing her uniform, sat in her place and ate a meal, for which I was extremely grateful. I was just coming back, to return Ailsa's uniform to her in the nurses' residence when I met the Senior Nursing Sister.
>
> 'Oh, Nurse Bennett,' she said, 'I was wondering why you tilt the bottom of your bed up at night?' This was a habit of Ailsa's. 'It's my legs, Sister,' I said. 'They get uncomfortable at night. I find raising the foot of the bed, so that my ankles are higher than my hips, relieves the discomfort.' This was true of Ailsa, and was an ongoing problem she had, which later developed into varicose veins. The sister continued to walk alongside me whilst we discussed 'my' strange habit,

and as we entered my sister's bedroom, who do you think was sitting on the bed?'

'Who are you? Who are you?' Poor Sister asked each of us. She appeared completely bewildered, so we had to confess. I explained 'Actually we're sisters. I'm a student of physiotherapy and I borrowed her clothes so that I could have a meal.' The Sister was very understanding possibly because I looked as if I was just so extremely hungry!'

Sheila continued to be very physically active, still playing tennis and cycling everywhere, and consequently food was never far from her mind. During her training in Orpington, she and her friend Mary Gude had their lectures in a nearby mansion house in the mornings and then did practical work in Orpington Hospital in the afternoons. One Friday, after her lectures, Sheila left a window unlocked, with the idea that she would return on the Saturday with Mary and they would try to cook themselves something to eat. Sheila takes up the story:

'The following Saturday I scaled up the drainpipe, got in through the open window, and went down to let Mary in. She went into the library and turned on one of the radiators – fortunately they were the old-fashioned kind, with bars that lit up with the heat – then laid it on its side and put some bread on the top of the grid to make toast. Meanwhile I was in another room doing the same thing, but with a pan. I was scrambling some eggs, or rather I had got some powdered egg which I was mixing, hoping to make something resembling scrambled eggs. We were just ready to start putting it on plates when I heard 'crunch-crunch-crunch' on the driveway leading up to the front door. I looked out and there was the Matron of Guy's Hospital walking up the steps with Sister, the head of the Physiotherapy Department. As they opened the front door, we heard Matron say, 'Do you smell toast?' I knew the game was up and that I had to step forward and show myself. When they asked me what I was doing, I replied 'Well Matron, if I am to survive this course, I'll definitely have to eat more. I've spent so many weeks being hungry, that I decided that I would have to come and make myself a meal. So I was just about to eat scrambled eggs on toast when you arrived.'

'So where is this meal?' she asked. 'Oh dear,' I said. 'Unfortunately, in my panic, I rushed into the bathroom and turned the pan upside down into the bath. The bad news is that the bath was full of water for fire watching and now the scrambled egg is sailing around on the top of the water.' 'I see,' she said. 'And where is the toast?' 'I don't know,' I answered. 'I'll have to ask my friend where the toast is.' So Mary stepped out and said, 'I was in the library and I've just put the toast behind the books.'

Matron knew my name and she knew I had a sister who was nursing, so I was worried that there would be serious repercussions to our actions, and that my course would be put in jeopardy. However, instead of being annoyed and having us disciplined in some way, she must have realized we were genuinely starving to have gone to such extremes, and the incident was never referred to again.'

Sheila was born with a naturally enquiring mind and a thirst for knowledge. Throughout her life, both professional and personal, she has sought information and explanation, learned new skills, and when she has not been provided with an adequate answer she has devised her own solutions. The hospital in Orpington was a rich source of medical knowledge, not only for nurses, but also medical staff and medical students. However whilst nurses were allowed to observe operations, and sometimes permitted to attend lectures intended for medical staff and students, the physiotherapy students were not offered these opportunities.

Sheila solved this problem by characteristically coming up with her own solution, which was to again request the loan of Ailsa's nursing uniform. Posing as a nurse, Sheila was able to observe many operations, which she not only found fascinating but which afforded her a crucial understanding of how the body – limbs, joints, muscles, ligaments and so forth – is constructed. One day she saw that a Greek surgeon, by the name of Mr Lambrinudi, who was a member of

Guy's staff and was renowned for his research into feet, was visiting Orpington.

'I saw on a notice board that he was to be showing a film and giving a lecture to qualified medical people only, and students were not invited. However I was determined that I was going to it so, when everyone else was seated, I crept in and sat on the end of a bench at the back. Mr Lambrinudi took off his shoes and showed that the way his foot moved was in fact, exactly the same as the way he used his fingers. He had had a carpenter carve an exact replica of each of the bones of the foot, and then he had used string to replace the tendons linking the bones. When you pulled certain strings, you got a sort of puppet show and in this way he was able to demonstrate the cause of certain deformities of the foot.

In the middle of the lecture, I heard him say 'I think we'll have a break for tea before we have the second half and I will ask the student to make the tea.' He looked directly at me, so I got up, went into the kitchen, made tea and brought it out to everyone. He obviously made it clear to me that he had known that I shouldn't have been there, but he didn't ask me to leave, so I sat down and remained for the second half. Both the lecture and the film were fascinating and based entirely on his own research – it was so kind of him to allow me to stay. Sometime later, I was to study under him and accompany him on ward rounds. Based on his research, Mr Lambrinudi introduced an operation on the ankle and foot which helped many patients, and which I was fortunate to observe being performed by another surgeon in the late 1950's. However although his work was innovative at the time, I do not believe they are still performing Lambrinudi operations.'

In 1944 a new surgical instrument was being introduced which was a small rotary saw, set on a long handle. It had a blade which rotated at high speed, to be used for cutting into bone. Sheila remembers that a patient of hers was to be having bone grafts to his spine and Mr Lambrinudi was using this new instrument for the first time.

'I can remember this so well, I can even tell you that it was a Thursday. I heard later that, during the operation, he dropped the saw and opened the patient right up his back. Fortunately they were able to utilize the help of a number of other surgeons to successfully repair the patient. Mr Lambrinudi went home straight after the operation, and was sadly found later that afternoon dead in his chair having suffered a massive stroke in the morning. This was the reason he had dropped the saw – his hand had become suddenly paralysed in the moment of the stroke.'

Shortly before Sheila left Guy's, her habit of observing operations by impersonating a nurse, was to get her into a serious situation, which potentially threatened her career. As she explains:

'I had changed into theatre scrubs to watch the operation, and I had returned to the changing room to put on my physiotherapy uniform, when Mr Batchelor, the surgeon in charge, came in. 'Oh, Nurse Bennett,' he said, thinking I was Ailsa. 'Don't leave yet. We have an emergency coming in.' In hindsight, that was the time I should have admitted who I was, but instead I went back into the theatre, and this gentleman was brought in having been in a road traffic accident, and who was going to have his leg amputated. The first thing, Mr Batchelor asked me for was a bucket, and luckily I knew what a bucket was, but not where to find it! Eventually I did come across one, but as the operation continued, the other nurses who didn't know who I was could not understand what was happening because, obviously, I was pretty useless. I slipped away as fast as I could after the operation ended.

Shortly after that I left Guy's and went to work in the Southern General Hospital in Dartford. I'd only been there a short time when I was asked to make up the numbers in an all-male hockey match, because otherwise the team couldn't have played their Saturday game. The field was very muddy and I slipped, my leg went underneath me and 'crack'! When I arrived back at the hospital, I was waiting for the visiting surgeon, and who should walk in but Mr Batchelor. He picked up my leg and looked at me, 'We have met before,' he said.

'Yes,' I said, agreeing with him. No other words were exchanged. He did what he could for me and was absolutely marvelous. There had been no need for me to confess I believe he had always known.'

As previously mentioned, Sheila has always led a very active life, and this love of exercise and her adventurous spirit have been the cause of quite a number of accidents over the years. During her time as a student she would cycle everywhere, including to and from the hospital every day and in her first year, aged about 19, she had an accident which involved a bicycle, a tennis racquet, a railway crossing and a heap of coal. Sheila takes up the story:

'One day, I was going to be playing tennis after I had finished my day at the hospital, so I had to take my racquet with me. I was going down a steep hill holding my tennis racquet in my hand. At the bottom of the hill there was a level crossing, and when I was about half way down, I noticed the gates were closing because a train was coming. Unfortunately when I tried to brake, the handle of my tennis racquet got between the brake and the handlebars and I couldn't stop. All I could do, before I hit the barrier, was swerve to the left where there was an alleyway with a coal heap which had been shunted there by one of the trains. My bike hit the coal heap and I went flying over the handlebars and landed on top of it. I knocked out all my front teeth, and I've still got coal in my knee from that endeavour. It wasn't a disaster though because Guy's had a first class dental department.

Of course, being wartime, there was the blackout to contend with too, which of course included a ban on bicycle

lights. One night I was trying to return to my digs in the
dark and I couldn't see a thing. I hit a wall, went right over
the top and landed amongst the hens in the local poultry
farm. I'd imagine they had quite a fright too, because
they all started panicking and squawking, as I landed in
the middle of them. I was injured this time, but only a
few cuts and bruises, nothing broken, so I just got myself
up and carried on.'

Naturally, amongst all her adventures, Sheila was studying very hard
to achieve her goal of qualifying as a physiotherapist. She counts
many friends as helping her along the way, not just her fellow
students, but sometimes the patients themselves. In her final year at
Guy's, by now in London, she met a patient Ada Ferrin who worked
for the McVities biscuit company, and used to regularly supply
Sheila with bags of rejected broken biscuits and dented tins – a very
welcome gift, during the war, to a student with an insatiable appetite
for exercise and food. Ada lived with her friend, Effie Hiscott, and
the three of them became lifelong friends. Sheila would spend the
weekends at their house in Surrey, where they would go for long
walks and picnics, but also where Sheila would spend a lot of time
studying for her exams.

Sheila knows how fortunate she has always been to have such a
retentive memory but she adds:

'I'm also lucky enough to have a photographic memory and
on top of all that I've had a great deal of luck. For instance
the day I was travelling up to London to take my finals, I
felt confident that I had covered the entire curriculum, but
as I was glancing through my anatomy book, I came across
a diagram of the thorax, a subject which had not been
part of my studies. That afternoon I took my written exam
and afterwards I had to attend an oral exam, where the
examiner had my written paper in front of him. If you got
high marks on your written paper, then the examiner would
ask you different questions on related subjects not covered
in the curriculum to see, whether or not, they would award
you a distinction.

I was the last student to be examined and the examiner said to me, 'I would like you to draw the surface markings of lymph drainage of the thorax,' which I was able to do because I had seen it in the book whilst on the train. However after looking at my diagram, the examiner told me that my diagram was wrong but that he would give me a chance to correct it. I said 'Thank you very much for the chance, but I cannot change it because I believe I am right, so I don't know what to do.' Again he said it was wrong and that I had one more chance to correct it, but I had to repeat that I could not see how I could alter it as I believed it to already be correct. There was another examiner over on the other side of a screen questioning another student, so my examiner said to his colleague 'My student is telling me that her answer is correct. I'm giving her the chance to change it so will you please tell her the correct answer.' 'Let me see what she's done,' the other examiner said. After he had looked at my diagram, he smiled and said 'The student is right.'

I thought proving the examiner wrong would work against me, but he must have gracefully accepted the fact because I received distinction in every single section of my exams. I think most people would have been swayed and re-examined their answer, but I knew I had the right one because I had learnt to trust my memory, but it was also a remarkable stroke of luck to be asked the exact thing I had just looked at.'

However Sheila did have a worrying moment the weekend her final exam results were announced. She had already taken up a position at the Naval Hospital in Dartford on the personal recommendation of the Matron of Guy's and as she was cycling back from visiting Ada and Effie in Surrey, she called in to pick up another student so that they could cycle back together to the hospital. As Sheila cycled into the garden of the house she was sharing with other young colleagues, her friend put her head out of the top floor window and shouted 'Our results are out'. Sheila shouted back 'Have you passed?' and her friend replied 'Yes!' Sheila then asked 'Have I passed?' but her friend disappeared back inside the house without saying anything, so Sheila presumed that it was bad news. However once inside the house, to Sheila's relief, her friend confirmed that Sheila had also passed, and the two of them cycled back to the Naval hospital together. Sheila describes the moment she walked into her room at the hospital:

'It was covered in flowers, telegrams, every mortal thing you could imagine and I couldn't understand it at all. There were telegrams for me from all sorts of people, including a lot of the other students. The results had been out for a day or two, but I had missed them because I'd been staying with Ada and Effie. It turned out that, in addition to getting a Distinction in my finals, I had also come top in Great Britain out of three hundred and forty five people who took their finals that year. This meant that Guy's was also first on the list and it was the first time any Guy's student had done that. The Matron of Guy's, the same one who uncovered the scrambled eggs and toast incident, sent me a telegram saying 'Congratulations! Guy's is now first.'

I felt that I had gone some way to making up for our disastrous attempt at cooking.'

Chapter 5

As with many areas of medicine, physiotherapy developed enormously during the Second World War due to the wide ranging injuries of the huge number of casualties brought home to hospitals and temporary hospitals desperate for help so that they could return to their families and live productive lives. The sheer scale of the injuries that the medical staff were faced with encouraged many to try to be innovative in their ideas of how to treat their patients, Sheila included. She had already experienced how valuable an innovative approach could be whilst she had been training and been able to observe Mr Lambrinudi and his progress with the study of the foot. However she had also assisted another pioneering doctor, an orthopaedic surgeon by the name of Major T.T. Stamm, whose interest lay in the construction of human joints. He had been motivated by one of his patients, a sixteen year-old girl called Nina, whose hip joints had never formed properly and so she had been unable to walk since birth. As Sheila explains:

> 'Major Stamm decided that, in some way, he had to replace
> Nina's hip joints and thus decided that he would have
> to make the ball and socket joint himself, out of what I
> presumed to be bone from the bone bank in the hospital.
> This he did and then replaced one of her hips with the
> artificial joint, and became the first person in the world
> to successfully introduce the hip replacement operation.
> Major Stamm undertook all Nina's physiotherapy himself,
> moving her appropriately, and so forth. Within two years,
> Major Stamm had replaced Nina's other hip joint and

eventually managed to get her standing and walking. He also had a portable flight of steps made and then taught her to climb them. I was lucky enough to witness him moving Nina in these very specific exercises. Having written his paper, Major Stamm then travelled to many different countries, taking Nina with him, demonstrating artificial hip joints. This was ten years before any hip joint was replaced in this country. Naturally today a hip replacement is a common and mostly routine operation which often benefits the recipient no end, removing pain and increasing their mobility and of course the range of modern materials available means the operations have a high level of success.

It was exciting to be involved in the vanguard of a profession, and I believe it was witnessing this necessity for invention, which has influenced the way I have always worked and still do so today. Years of experience have taught me to recognize when I am unable to help a patient, but I also know that a combination of inventiveness and sheer determination can work wonders. With a clear understanding of the mechanics of the body, I have devised many of my own exercises or pieces of equipment for clients with specific needs, often with very successful results.

In addition to the war providing us with a great number of patients, polio was still rife in Britain and we had to learn how to counteract the effects of it on our patients, many of them young children.'

Sheila's first job, after she qualified, was in a Naval Hospital in Dartford which held a large number of British troops who had been captured by the Japanese and imprisoned for some considerable time in the Japanese Prisoner of War camps. These men were severely physically deformed because they had been held for very lengthy periods in extremely confined spaces, unable to straighten their limbs.

As a result of this confinement and other cruel treatment by their Japanese captors, many patients were also mentally disturbed and unstable, often suffering hallucinations and engaging in violent behaviour towards themselves and others. Many committed suicide and one of Sheila's patients who was allowed home on Christmas Day, killed his mother in a psychotic rage, demonstrating how unstable the patients, with whom Sheila and her colleagues were working in close contact with on a daily basis, were.

The hospital was made up of a number of buildings, of which one was designated the living quarters for these ex prisoners-of-war. Although they were known to be dangerous, their building could never be locked, because the medical staff believed that the patients' reaction to being confined again, might trigger some sort of homicidal rage, which would have caused them to turn on each other. Thus these highly dangerous and unpredictable patients had to be allowed to roam freely outside, wandering around the grounds of the hospital. These were the conditions Sheila and her fellow staff worked in as they tried to help those who had returned from the war with such terrible debilitating injuries, both physical and mental. Sheila explains more of her time at Dartford:

'My colleagues and I had to walk through the grounds of the hospital as we went from our residence to the department, and many of the staff were understandably afraid of those who had been prisoners of war of the Japanese. However I did not feel so intimidated, as I was tall at five foot ten inches and I was also physically fit and strong from all my exercise. If one of the patients wanted our attention, he would crash a crutch against the staff room door, which would cause the other three members of the physiotherapy department, all of whom were rather small to become anxious and worried about what was to happen next. I never had the slightest qualms. I knew I had to govern the situation from the start, so I would open the door and command them to enter the department. Having taken them in, I would treat them and was never concerned that any of them would hurt me and they never did. Some people can get nervous in situations like that, but I found that by being in charge at the beginning, the patients wouldn't take over or act up. Perhaps it had something to do with their conditioning to obey orders from a commanding officer.'

The first job for the physiotherapists was to begin by helping their patients to straighten out the limbs which were so contracted and deformed. As Sheila soon observed, their physical deformities could have been alleviated if someone in the camp had thought to lie the soldiers on their backs and straighten their limbs in the air, changing position until each joint had been put through its full range of motion. Not only was this now physically difficult for the patients, but these simple exercises had to be continuously repeated, and many found it difficult to concentrate or remain motivated. Sheila soon took her own view of what she felt her patients were most in need of:

'Because the soldiers were in such a state, they needed someone to be firm with them, and to persevere day and night. If the physio persists then the patient will do it, but you've got to be prepared to be the driving force to get everyone going and keep them going.

'Lie on your back,' I used to tell them. 'Bend and stretch but keep going!'

Once they got going and continued to do the exercises, their physical condition would improve enormously and of course this often had a very positive effect on their mental well-being.'

During Sheila's time at Dartford, she was resident with a therapist by the name of Joan Driver who was to become a lifelong friend. Joan was blind from birth and had qualified at the Institute of Blind Physiotherapists, before beginning her job at Dartford. One day she expressed her regret to Sheila that she could never receive any private correspondence from her sighted friends, because, of course all her letters had to read aloud to her. With her usual generosity and enthusiasm, Sheila decided that she would learn Braille so that she would be able to communicate directly with Joan when they eventually left the hospital. At that time it was a very complicated process, which involved using a special hand tool to press the paper to create the Braille dots. As the person receiving the letter would have to turn the paper over to 'read' the words, it meant that the composer of the letter had to write in reverse, from right to left and upside down, which sounds incredibly complicated but, according to

Sheila, 'Once you've got the hang of it, it's actually quite easy.' It took Sheila six months of studying and practising before she passed her qualification in writing Braille, delighting Joan who would always remain grateful for her thoughtfulness.

After two years in the Naval Hospital, Sheila saw an advert for a three-year contract in Bulawayo, Rhodesia and decided to apply:

'Tennis had stopped altogether in Britain, but the full effects of the war had not reached Rhodesia, and I knew that if I went, there would be plenty of opportunity to play again. Unfortunately I had to be twenty five for the job and I was two years short of that, but I decided to apply anyway. I received an invitation to an interview, and reasoned that I may as well combine the trip to London with meeting up with some friends afterwards for a picnic. Consequently I did not arrive in particularly formal attire, believing this to be the first in what would surely be a series of interviews, and was somewhat dismayed to be confronted by an enormous board of examiners. They all closely studied my qualification certificates, and grilled me relentlessly with dozens of questions, before asking me to wait outside whilst they continued interviewing the other candidates.

Whilst I was waiting, a lady came out and asked me to take a letter to a doctor in Harley Street, who would assess my physical condition. After the examination the doctor declared me to be the fittest person he had ever seen. I explained to him that whilst I was at the Naval Hospital, and after having done a full day's work, I would cycle eleven miles every night, there and back, to go and pick fruit on a fruit farm to supplement my wages. I explained to him that we were paid for the quantity of fruit we were able to pick. One evening I arrived at the farm just as a doodle bug landed in the orchard next door and the blast was such that it nearly blew me over, but it also took all the plums off the trees – all I had to do was pick them up and put them into baskets. I earned a tremendous amount that day. The Harley Street doctor

laughed and said, 'You are going to enjoy Rhodesia.'
'Enjoy Rhodesia?' I replied, 'I don't even know if I am
going.' 'I can tell you that you are,' he replied. 'They've
selected you and you will be there in a fortnight.'

No one had asked me my age and so I hadn't told them
– it was only when I arrived in Rhodesia that they found
out. The doctor was right – within a fortnight I left the
Naval Hospital and travelled straight to the docks, to board
a ship for South Africa. I didn't even get time to go home
to say cheerio to my family.

The first person I met on board was a lady by the name
of Constance Pooley, who had been interviewed at the same
time as me for a position in the Maternity Department of
the same hospital. She had noticed that I had been dressed
for a picnic at the interview and as we laughed about it
I knew that I had made a firm friend. We were very close
for the three years I was there, and when she married
and remained in South Africa, I became Godmother to
her daughter Judy who was born after I had left. Judy is
still in South Africa and has three daughters of her own
now. She still remembers visiting me in England when
she was seven and she saw snow for the first time. I am
delighted to say that we have kept in touch and remain
close, after all these years.'

Chapter 6

At the tender age of twenty three, Sheila found herself in charge of the Physiotherapy Department of Bulawayo General Hospital in Rhodesia which mainly treated Europeans. Many of the staff were older than Sheila and all highly experienced, but Sheila was to find that experience did not necessarily equate with care and efficiency:

'There was a physio in my department who was much older than me and it soon became clear that she resented my authority. I, in turn, did not believe that she was particularly good with the patients, and I could never actually trust that she was giving them proper treatment. I soon found out that she was shirking her duties, and amusing herself rather than doing her job. Of course when I found her out she wasn't pleased at all and when she left shortly after, she said to me 'I've never disliked anybody as much as I dislike you.' 'Really?' I replied 'That's most interesting because usually a feeling isn't mutual, but it is in this instance.'

I have never taken anything said to me personally. People can say what they like about me and that is their opinion, and who's to say which opinion is right? I find that my nature suits me extraordinarily well to live with and I always try to make the best out of everything. The people who come to me for treatment have always found me exactly the same – I've never had a cross word with anybody who's been in my house.'

During her time in Rhodesia, Sheila and her staff treated mostly accidents and injuries and dealt with the disabilities caused by polio which was rampant at that time. As Sheila was resident in the hospital she would often treat her patients throughout the weekends, as well as during the week. One such patient was an eight year-old girl called Alma, who was totally paralysed and confined to a spinal carriage, which was a type of wheeled hospital bed with sides on which she was transported. During the two years that Sheila treated Alma, she was able to get her standing and beginning to walk and at the weekends, Sheila would visit her at home to teach her different skills to practise with her hands.

'That year, King George and Queen Elizabeth, the present Queen's parents, visited Rhodesia in the 'Ivory Train' – so called because of its colour. During their visit to the Matopas Hills, they were arriving at a nearby station, so I took Alma along to see them. The Queen saw us and immediately came over and started chatting. Poor Alma was so overwhelmed that she was completely unable to say anything!

Forty years later, I received a letter from Alma, which began 'I only hope this letter reaches the right person.' It turned out that she had been writing letters for years and years trying to reach me to thank me. She told me that although she was still severely handicapped, she was employed in the railway office, and was able to get about using a specially converted car given to her by the Rhodesian Rotary Club. I wrote back and told her all that had happened to me in the intervening years, and she said that the one thing she wanted to do in life was to meet me again. Unfortunately due to her health that never managed to take place and she died about 5 years later.'

Due to the unrest and the violent clashes between the authorities and the local population at that time, many of Sheila's patients were members of the British South African Police Force. Sheila knew she was a hard task master but she also knew that her methods worked:

'One Monday morning, I went into the department and on the outside of the door, there was an enormous placard which read, 'Abandon hope all ye who enter here,' signed the B.S.A.P. Below was a picture of a soldier all bandaged up with an arm out to one side and his leg up in the air, and a caption which read 'We'll start with an easy one.' It was a skit on me giving them such difficult exercises. I knew I was tough on them, but they needed me to be, and when they saw the benefits, they began to enjoy it. As I was resident, I would also spend a lot of off-duty time with them as well, and they appreciated that and would certainly try their best, and to work as hard as they could.'

At that time, the tension between the local black population and the whites made life in Rhodesia unpredictable and often dangerous. Whilst Sheila was there, there was a strike by the black servants and many began to attack their employers. Although Sheila and her staff were never attacked, there was one tense night when the black staff surrounded the home of the head of the hospital, intending to murder him and his family. Fortunately the troops arrived in time and were able to escort them to safety.

After a while staying in residence in the hospital, Sheila moved to live outside the city to experience more of the beauty and relative peacefulness of the countryside. One day she and three friends decided to drive out to a local beauty spot known for the stunning waterfall. Whilst admiring the view Sheila noticed an unusual bark pattern on one of the trees partially hidden amongst the dense vegetation, and declared that she would like to take a closer look. Her friends were not very enthusiastic and pointed out the nearby sign which stated 'DANGEROUS ANIMALS. DO NOT GET OUT OF YOUR VEHICLE.' Sheila replied 'I'll only be a second – you all know that I can move pretty quickly if I need to.' and proceeded to get out of the car and move towards the tree. As she got closer to it she could see how beautiful the pattern was and when she stroked the bark, it felt almost velvety. As she looked around she realized that she was surrounded by four tree trunks all with the same pattern, and she reached up to stroke the branch above her head which she assumed was part of the same tree. It was at this point that one of the 'trees' suddenly lifted up and was replaced on the ground, and when Sheila looked up above the trees, she could make out the head of the giraffe whose tummy she appeared to be tickling. Although she moved at some speed back to the safety of the car, her experience left her with a lifelong fascination for these graceful animals.

Nearby to Sheila's new accommodation lived Miss Bavin whose job Sheila had taken over on her retirement from the Physiotherapy Department in the hospital. Miss Bavin had retired to a beautiful estate where she spent much of her time looking after her string of ponies, and as Sheila had ridden extensively as a child, she was thrilled when Miss Bavin offered her the opportunity to do so again.

'We used to ride out into the bhundu which is dehydrated sand really, with the odd Monkey Puzzle tree and cacti. Sometimes we would spend all morning riding out to a shack, where we would have a picnic lunch, and then ride all the way home again. Before we set off we would groom the horses, which I was doing one day, when I heard 'Chomp, chomp.' and realized that the hungry pony was eating the brim of my straw sun hat. As well as a lot of riding, I was also able to play a lot of tennis, with some very fine players, and make some new friends, so I was lucky to achieve what I had hoped to.

Eventually the time came when I had run the department for 3 years, and although I was proud of how it had grown, I had grown tired of the limited challenge of treating polio and injuries at an all European hospital. I decided that I would return to England, to Guy's Hospital to qualify as a teacher of 'Electricity Training', which was a relatively new area at the time, but which is more familiar today. It involved special machines which were the forerunners to the TENS machines in use today, and which used electricity to treat various conditions such as circulatory problems, stimulating muscles and inflammatory ailments. On the way back to England I had to spend one night in Cape Town, before catching the boat the next day. During that one evening

I went for a walk near the Cape Town University and met someone who again would take me in a different direction to the one I had envisioned.'

Chapter 7

As Sheila was taking an evening stroll in Cape Town, she became aware of a distinguished looking gentleman, smiling at her and attempting to catch her attention. As a young lady, Sheila had very striking colouring, and her dark hair, piercing blue eyes, pale skin and pink cheeks of a classic English rose, caused her to stand out in South African society. As a result of this, she was quite used to people staring at her as she walked by, but on this occasion the gentleman in question stopped her and engaged her in conversation. He was Dr Harold Myers, who was on the staff of Cape Town University, second to the University Chancellor, Professor Forman. Dr Myers was obviously enamoured of Sheila and invited her to dinner that night, during which she explained who she was, and what her role had been at Bulawayo Hosptal. She also explained that she was returning to England for a well-deserved holiday before beginning the training to teach Medical Electricity.

Dr Myers, impressed by what he heard, asked Sheila if she would consider employment at Groote Schuur Hospital, the largest hospital in Cape Town, established for the care of the white and European population. Sheila was non-committal at the time explaining that she was keen to return home to see her family. However Dr Myers was clearly determined to entice Sheila out to South Africa again, and he was also a man with a strong social conscience, so with these two aims in mind, he wrote to Sheila in England and asked her to open a physiotherapy department in the hospital for the treatment of the less affluent locals, the blacks and other non-white patients, who were unable to get treatment in the white European clinic. Such an offer appealed to Sheila's generous nature and so she found herself once again travelling back to South Africa. One of her first tasks was to learn Afrikaans and with the benefit of evening classes, Sheila was soon able to communicate with her new patients and began to enjoy her new job. As Sheila's patients were not charged for their treatment, they repaid her kindness by regularly bringing her gifts, and Sheila soon made many new friends. Dr Myers however was also keen for Sheila's attention and within a few days of her arrival he visited her clinic with an invitation to accompany him to meet the former South African Prime Minister, General Smuts. As Sheila remembers of that time:

'Dr Myers was treating all the V.I.P.s in connection with the University in Cape Town and shortly after I arrived there, he invited me to accompany him on a visit to General Smuts, a military leader and philosopher who was twice Prime Minister of South Africa. General Smuts was eighty when I met him, and had recently suffered a heart attack. He was staying in the Mount Nelson, one of the largest hotels in Capetown, to convalesce. The University was naturally contacted and Dr Myers was asked to attend him. 'Come along with me, and I'll introduce you,' Dr Myers said to me. I'd only been in Cape Town two days and I was wearing a bright blue velvet jacket and, of course, in those days I had bright pink cheeks and very dark hair. When I met General Smuts in his room at the Mount Nelson, he looked at me and said, 'You're not South African – not with colouring like that.' Obviously his eyesight was still very good. 'No,' I replied. 'I've just arrived from British soil'.

General Smuts was given strict instructions about what he could and couldn't do to aid his recovery, one of which was not to climb the stairs – he was to always use the lift.

General Smuts followed instructions and was doing extraordinarily well for the first fortnight, but then there was suddenly a downturn in his health. When Dr Myers went to see him, General Smuts explained that he was a member of the very prestigious club, the Mountain Club of South Africa, whose elite members had to climb Table

Mountain, which is just over 1000 metres high, every month to retain their membership, so although he had followed the instruction not to climb the stairs, he had climbed Table Mountain because according to him 'No one told me not to.' General Smuts's condition deteriorated and he was taken home to his farm at Irene in Pretoria, where he died shortly afterwards. I attended his memorial service which was held, appropriately enough, on the top of Table Mountain, having scaled the heights myself, along with four thousand others.

I climbed Table Mountain several times after that, and on one November 5th night we stayed in one of the Mountain Club's chalets, right on the very top so that we could look down on to the fireworks below. My friend and I decided to try to get closer to the edge of the mountain so that we could see the fireworks more clearly, but the battery in our torch failed and we were plunged into complete darkness. We knew there were 12 reservoirs of water on the top of the mountain and we didn't think that we'd ever get back without plunging into water or falling down the mountainside. Fortunately we found our way back, and now of course they have railways going up and down the mountain.'

At this time, Sheila was again able to indulge her love of tennis, and found a lot of other enthusiasts at the Western Province Club, one of the most prestigious clubs in Cape Town. Although she played both doubles and singles, it was singles she excelled at. Prior to Sheila's arrival, the ladies singles title had been held by a lady by the name of Margo McMorland for the previous four years, so it was a surprise for everyone when Sheila soundly beat her in the final, 6–2, 6–1. As they walked off court, Margo said 'What a pity the score did not reflect how level the match was.' They became great friends and were able to laugh about this later on. Sheila is still in regular contact with Margo's daughter, Ann, who most recently visited Sheila in July 2015, to reminisce and laugh about the infamous tennis match.

Despite these moments of levity, it was important to remember that Cape Town was still a very dangerous place, with a great deal of unrest between the whites and the locals. Within weeks of her arrival, Sheila was making the return journey to her digs which consisted of a bus ride followed by a short walk. It was still daylight, and her flat which was upstairs was accessed by going up an outside flight of stairs. As she was walking from the bus-stop, Sheila became aware of a large black man closely following her. As she picked up her pace, so did he:

> 'I realized I was being chased, and I knew that I had to make it to the stairs and then up them with my key ready, otherwise if he'd followed me up the stairs, he could get me at the top whilst I fumbled for my key. In fact I was much faster than him, which he soon realized and so he stopped chasing me. It was a very frightening experience and one which taught me that I should never go anywhere on my own again. It was only because I was so fit from playing tennis that I was able to outrun him.'

Towards the end of her time in Cape Town, Sheila was again witness to the immense dangers of living in South Africa during this turbulent time in its history. At that time, there was a notorious area situated just outside Cape Town which was known as 'District 6'. District 6 was populated solely by black and Afrikaans people and other non-white immigrants, many of whom were living in severe poverty, and also many who were violent and particularly hostile towards the white population. For this reason District 6 was designated a 'no go' zone for white skinned individuals, as they were attacked and often killed as soon as they entered this area regardless of their often charitable intentions.

There was, however, one Afrikaans lady on the hospital staff who had built a strong rapport with many of the residents of District 6 and was able to move freely in and out of the area, offering help and medical assistance. She and Sheila had become friends during their time working together and one day she asked Sheila to accompany her into District 6 to witness, for herself, the appalling conditions under which these people were living. Sheila was understandably wary of entering the area having heard all the stories of violence, but this lady was very confident in her own influence and assured Sheila that she would be perfectly safe under her protection. They set off in this lady's car and Sheila knew as soon as they entered District 6 that they had severely misjudged the situation:

'I remember the moment we started driving into the District. Just the sight of a white person in the car was enough to enrage the populace and without any warning, we were immediately surrounded by an angry mob of black locals who clambered all over the car and started smashing the car and the windows.

It was absolutely terrifying and I was convinced that I was yet another European who had entered District 6, but who wasn't going to leave it alive. Fortunately my friend was eventually able to calm the situation enough for us to drive out at some speed. As well as a terrifying experience, it must have been mortally disappointing for my friend. She had spent many hours trying to build relationships with these people and helping them when she was able, and she honestly believed that she held a position of respect, at least enough to be assured that neither she nor anyone with her would ever be attacked. I do not believe she ever entered District 6 again and in fact, she left South Africa not long after that.'

Life for white Europeans in South Africa in the 1940s was immensely limiting due to the simmering tension between the whites and the non-whites which exploded daily into violence. The threat of attack was constant and Sheila began to find the many security arrangements that were necessary very restrictive. She also began to find her work less rewarding, as she spent more and more of her time treating Europeans who had been injured whilst caught up in the violence, which had not been the original purpose of her role. She also realized that she did not wish to accept Dr Myers's proposal of marriage, or to remain in Cape Town, and so began to make plans to return to Britain.

The first task for Sheila was to help to find the replacement who would take on her position as head of the Department of Physiotherapy at Groote Schuur after she had left. Of those who applied for this prestigious position, one was a young lady from Switzerland named

Miss Pfister whom the interviewing board refused to employ because she did not have an English Certificate of Qualification, despite having all the relevant Swiss qualifications. Sheila, however, knew Miss Pfister, and had worked with her and heartily disagreed with the Board's decision:

'I raised Heaven and Earth for that young lady to take my place, because I knew her and I knew she was an excellent physio, and I didn't think the English Certificate made the slightest difference to her ability to run the department. After various 'heated discussions', I managed to persuade the board to employ her. She was terribly grateful, and when I left, she gave me a book with an inscription inside: 'I shall never forget your kindness. Perhaps one day I shall have the opportunity of thanking you.' I was very touched at the time but doubted if we would ever see each other again. I was wrong and we were to meet again under extraordinary circumstances.

When it came time to board the ship which was to take me back to England, I was astonished to find that I was sharing the cabin with a lady four years my senior, who was also a physiotherapist. Fate again had taken a hand in my future, as this lady was to give me some excellent advice about what NOT to do next!'

Chapter 8

The physiotherapist Sheila met on the boat returning to England had also trained at Guy's and had just finished teaching at the University of Witwatersrand in Johannesburg. Coincidentally she had been teaching medical electricity, which was of course the subject which was of some interest to Sheila. Unfortunately it soon became clear to Sheila that her new acquaintance was unwell, and had suffered some sort of breakdown. Over the next few days, as they continued to get to know each other better, this lady did indeed mention that she had had a nervous breakdown, which she attributed to the difficulty of teaching medical electricity, rather than living in the challenging social conditions in South Africa at that time. When she learned that this was indeed the same area that Sheila had intended to train in, she became very agitated and insisted that Sheila reconsider her decision, citing her own health as reason enough. Obviously such a heartfelt and spirited plea did cause Sheila to question her decision, and it was during this time on board ship that she was to receive a ship's cable from her old friend Mary Gude. Mary and Sheila had been great friends at Guy's and it was Mary who had been Sheila's accomplice in the 'scrambled eggs on toast' debacle. Before moving to South Africa, Sheila had spent many weekends with her friend in Bognor where Mary had started her own physiotherapy practice. A few days before Sheila began her journey back to Great Britain Mary had contacted Sheila, to inform her that her own brother had been seriously injured in a car crash in Cape Town:

'Mary had contacted the Chartered Society of
Physiotherapists to see if there was anybody she knew

in the Cape who would treat him. My name came up
and so she sent me a telegram asking if I would look
after her brother Ronnie. I was just days from boarding
the boat to come home to England, so I sent Mary a
telegram explaining that although I couldn't help as I
was returning to the UK, I had found someone else who
could, and sent her the contact details. Half way through
the voyage, I received a ship's cable from Mary: 'Consider
private practice Bognor.'

During the time Sheila had been working in Dartford and then South
Africa, Mary had married, had two children, and had also established
a very successful physiotherapy practice – so successful in fact that
she was unable to cope with the amount of work. She was of the
opinion that Sheila would be of great help to her if she also started a
practice in Bognor, and with immense generosity of spirit, she sought
to help Sheila as much as possible.

'Whilst on board the boat, I made the decision to accept
Mary's kind offer and tried to organize as much as possible
from the boat, including buying all the equipment I would
need, and a car to travel to patients. Mary was of course
an immense help and arranged some digs for me in Bognor
with a good friend of hers, Rachel Anderson, which would
also be suitable for me to run my clinic from. Within ten
days of landing in England, and a break to catch up with
my family whom of course I hadn't seen for a year and
a half, I moved into my new home in Bognor and was
ready to treat my first patient. My practice was started.
Unfortunately Mary died tragically young at the age of
fifty four from a brain tumour, but I will never forget her
generosity and help setting up my first practice. I think
Mary would be proud to know that I still have my own
practice today and I am still working.'

Five doors away from Sheila's home and practice, was the only
private medical practice in Bognor, run by a gentleman by the name
of Dr Gordon Ferres. Dr Ferres was very relieved to have another

physiotherapist to whom he could refer his patients, and between his referrals and the overspill from Mary's large practice, Sheila was soon extremely busy. As professional colleagues, Miss Bennett and Dr Ferres became friends, and it was not long before Sheila learnt that very sadly Dr Ferres's wife was in a nursing home having been diagnosed with a condition called Huntingdon's Chorea. This was a recently discovered condition, which was still, at that time difficult to diagnose. It was however known to be a genetic disease, passed down from a parent to a child. Dr Ferres's wife had been told, as a child, that her mother had died, but it was later revealed that she had not died but had been put into a nursing home with an undiagnosed condition, now obviously recognized as Huntingdon's Chorea. In fact her mother had lived into her seventies, remaining in the nursing home. As a fellow medical professional, Sheila was aware of the difficulties of having the disease, and was able to assist Dr Ferres to care for his wife in many ways, for instance by purchasing clothing or personal items on his behalf for his wife, or advising him on what she may need in the nursing home. Sadly Dr Ferres's wife died a short time later.

Prior to arriving in Bognor, Sheila had only worked in physiotherapy departments in hospitals, firstly the Naval Hospital in Dartford and then the hospitals in Rhodesia and South Africa, so she found running her own practice interesting and exciting:

'I had all different types of patients, of differing ages with a wide range of conditions being presented. I used to drive great distances travelling to neighbouring areas and on to many big estates and mansion houses, a bit like I have done in Banchory and the surrounding estates of Donside and Deeside. I met lots of fascinating and interesting people. The Duke and Duchess of Kent used to spend their holiday in Bognor and stayed two doors down from my lodgings. When they were there, they were looked after by Dr Ferres who introduced me one day.

In those days a treatment cost 7 shillings and sixpence, which was quite a lot at the time, so I was always keen to ensure that I could help my patients, and as I often travelled to their houses to treat them, I wasn't always sure of what I would find when I got there.

One day I was asked to treat a lady who lived on one of the more prestigious estates, comprising of some beautiful houses, and which had a gatekeeper whose job it was to vet those entering and leaving the estate. I explained who I was and gave the name of the lady I was to treat, and having established that I was telling the truth, the guard directed me to her house and let me on my way. As I parked my car, I noticed that the front door was slightly ajar. This in itself did not seem strange as it was a lovely sunny day, and indeed I also noticed that all the upstairs windows were open as well. As I got out of my car and began to walk up the path to the house, I heard the most magnificent singing, some coming out through the windows and some coming out of the open front door. For a few minutes, I just stood on the doorstep and savoured this magical moment. Eventually I couldn't wait any longer or I would have been very late for the appointment so I rang the doorbell. The young lady I had come to see, was soon to perform in the opera, *La Boheme*, and had been practising upstairs whilst waiting for me. However her mother was also an opera singer and had been practising downstairs. It was a sublime moment with the voices drifting out of the windows on the summer breeze.'

During her career, Sheila has treated many musicians of all types of instruments, including her own husband who was to become an accomplished violinist. However there is one patient whom she remembers with particular affection, and that was the renowned composer Eric Coates. Amongst his many famous compositions, Eric Coates was well known for composing the famous signature march theme of 'The Dam Busters' film around which the rest of the film score was based, and also 'By the Sleepy Lagoon' which is the signature tune to BBC Radio Four's 'Desert Island Discs' and at the time that Sheila knew him, he had just started writing commissions for the Royal Family. Eric Coates was a shy, private man, but he was also in great demand for publicity interviews or business discussions with, for instance, publishers of his music. As a result of this, he kept the downstairs of his house as a type of meeting area for more formal visits, whilst he himself lived upstairs in his private rooms where few people were allowed to enter. One of his rooms was a living room which was next door to his music room. As a composer, Eric Coates naturally spent a lot of time leaning over pianos and desks and so forth and consequently had problems with his arms and shoulders.

In order to treat any patient effectively, it is of immense use to Sheila to understand their working environment and how it might contribute to their condition. Consequently she was one of the very few people invited into Eric Coates living quarters.

'Very often, whilst I was treating him, he would suddenly say 'Oh, just a minute,' and he'd get up and walk next door to his music room. He'd sit down at his piano, and I would hear him tinkling away there, then he would come back and write something on his score, and I would then recommence treating him. At the time he was working on a piece of music called 'Elizabeth of Glamis' in honour of the late Queen Mother, mother of our present Queen Elizabeth II. The whole time I was treating him we had these interruptions for him to go and add something to the score, and then when I had finished we would have a dandelion coffee together.

Forty years later I was sitting in the grounds of Glamis Castle, listening to an open air concert of music by Eric Coates, to celebrate the Queen Mother's one hundredth birthday. Sadly he had already died by then at the age of seventy three, and I missed him enormously. It was one of the most moving experiences of my life, when they played 'Elizabeth of Glamis', and brought back those memories of him jumping up, going and adding this bit or that, and then coming back to me to continue his treatment.'

As with Eric Coates, Sheila has always started a new consultation by asking her patient a great many questions, not only about their condition, or what they are feeling, but also about their professions, what is happening at present, what has happened in the past, what they can do and what they can't. She maintains that she can almost always tell a patient's injuries before she has begun treating them by asking the right questions and listening intently to the answers and observing their movements. She calls her method of treatment, 'applied anatomy', and explains that it is logic based upon anatomy and the science of movement. She understands clearly how the body is supposed to move and what it should be able to do, and if a patient cannot achieve this on their own then she devises her own exercises to help them. As she explains:

'I decide what treatment to give my patients based upon real anatomy. I think about what they should be able to do, and if they can't, then I choose exercises accordingly. I remember, as a student, one of my examiners saying to me, 'In all the years that I have been an examiner, I have never come across a student who has devised more effective exercises than you for the condition we are dealing with.' I replied, 'To me it is just applied anatomy.'

Of course, my understanding of anatomy was greatly enhanced by my life as a keen sportswoman. I knew exactly what the human body was capable of, and how important belief is in yourself. If you're not particularly fit, or not interested in sport, you perhaps don't know what your body or your patient's ultimate capability is.

Then there is the importance of sheer determination. 'Concentrate, think, try, keep going,' is what I have always said to my patients even to this day. This too came from my life as a sportswoman and the determination to win was what drove me to succeed in games. I had to practise and practise and practise until I knew that I could win. Strangely I never took pleasure in beating an opponent, it was just my own accomplishment which was of importance to me. Soon, however, I had to learn the hardest lesson of my life, one which would challenge all of my professional beliefs.'

Chapter 9

It was Good Friday in 1953, and Sheila had been for a long walk with friends in the afternoon, prior to attending an appointment with a patient at her home, that evening. As she left the patient's house, and got back into her car, she had to reverse down a long narrow drive. Sheila struggled to turn her head and then realized that she was losing the feeling in her neck and that her neck was going 'floppy', and seemed unable to support the weight of her head. With all her past experience, Sheila suspected immediately that she had contracted polio. She was thirty years old, and a polio vaccine was just months away from being made widely available.

Sheila managed to drive her car the five miles to her lodgings, but was unable to get it into the garage. Having worked with many victims of polio, Sheila knew exactly what was happening to her and what the possible outcomes could be. She was already losing the use of her right arm, and knew that this was going to be the last day she would ever be fully active. Sheila also knew that the greatest threat in those early hours was if the polio affected her ability to breathe and knew that the coming hours may determine whether she lived or died:

> 'I put together all the records and everything relating to the practice, and got myself organised to be in hospital the following day. I was lucky enough to survive the night and when the doctor arrived the following morning, he noticed the book that I had happened to be reading lying on my bedside table. It was called 'Poliomyelitis' written by Ritchie Russell. He confirmed what I already knew, that it was

polio, and on the Saturday afternoon I was taken to
St. Richard's Hospital in Chichester. Of course the question
was asked of how I may have contracted the disease. I had
been treating a young lady for six months who did have
polio. Before her diagnosis, she had had twins who had
died at 2 weeks old of an undiagnosed condition. Shortly
after the funeral, the mother was diagnosed with polio,
and of course it was assumed that this is what had killed
the babies. Every time I went to treat her, I was scrupulous
about hygiene, always washing my hands on arriving and
leaving, but on just one occasion, I used her bathroom.
Afterwards it was found that the polio virus can survive
in a toilet for up to 6 months, so the doctors assumed that
this was where I had contracted it.

My landlady, Rachel had become a very dear friend
and kindly accompanied me to the hospital, bringing with
her a small bunch of flowers for me. After confirmation
of my diagnosis was made in the Outpatients Department,
I was to be placed in isolation in a room of my own. As I
have already mentioned, I am not easily offended or upset
– I accept that some people behave in a manner in which
I would not, but sometimes people's insensitivity can be
breathtaking. The nurse who was to wheel my bed into my
room, picked up both my lifeless arms, and crossed them
on my chest. She then picked up the little bunch of flowers
my landlady had left with me, placed them on my hands,
and said, 'Feet first for you,' which was another way of
saying that I was not going to survive. I recognized that
it was a terrible thing to say and do to a patient, greatly
insensitive, but fortunately, due to my own disposition, it
didn't upset me. I just shook it off and did not allow it to
upset me at all.

At ten o'clock that night, the door to my room opened
and it was the same nurse, but this time in floods of tears.
'I've come to apologise for what I did to you,' she said.
'Well,' I replied. 'You're lucky it was me you were so unkind
to. It meant nothing to me, didn't bother me at all. But tell
me, why have you come now?' 'Because this evening, my

own mother was admitted to Outpatients where she died.'
That would have been a very hard lesson for her, and
hopefully she learnt a lot that day. She hadn't upset me
because I just felt sorry for her that her nature was such
that she could actually do a thing like that. I have never
been disturbed by anything negative that anyone has said
to me – after all that is their opinion – but I have always
had confidence in my own philosophies and beliefs. I
honestly feel that this is another strength which my parents
gave to me. We always had to be very grateful for what we
had, and seek only to help others not hurt them.'

Chapter 10

The polio vaccine was introduced in 1953 for health workers, and by 1955, it was freely available to the public. Sheila contracted polio just a few months before she would have been eligible for the vaccine. She was only thirty years old. Polio has nearly been eradicated in the Western world but is still rife in Africa. It is a neurological disease, which damages the nerves in the spine, and it is the muscles which are related to these nerves which then become weakened and in some cases, completely unable to function.

Although Sheila knew immediately that she had contracted polio, she did not know how it would affect her or even whether it would prove fatal. The only certainty she had was that she would be severely disabled from that day forth. She faced the end of her career as a physiotherapist, the end of her sporting career including her beloved tennis and also knew that she would never again even be able to walk far. Sheila lost the use of her left leg, her right arm and the whole of her trunk, and the muscles of her head and neck were weakened as well. She was unable to sit up and spent seven months in hospital fighting the effects of the disease. During this time, she had five operations which included a full hysterectomy, ending any hope she had of having children. With her usual determination, Sheila tried to adopt an attitude of acceptance of her condition:

'I knew there was no point in wasting time and energy by being upset about the polio. The fact was, it had happened and my job was to make the best of it. In many ways it became an education because I learnt so much

55

trying to recover, and I was then able to use this experience later for the benefit of my patients.'

In fact Sheila was determined that she would use her experience to help her fellow physiotherapists to understand polio and the consequences of it to their patients by writing an article for the Journal of the Chartered Society of Physiotherapy. The introduction to the article states that the author 'Miss Sheila Bennett is a member of the Chartered Society and needs no further introduction to her fellow members', and the article itself is a record of not only Sheila's physical deterioration, but also how she coped mentally.

Whilst in hospital, Sheila shared a room with seven others including a lady called Edith Morel, who was the same age as Sheila and with whom Sheila would have a lifelong friendship. Edith had contracted polio in the W.R.N.S and suffered severe paralysis, which confined her to a wheelchair. Despite this, she still lives in Jersey and the two friends speak regularly on the telephone.

Although Sheila had enormous respect for the two New Zealand physiotherapists who tried to help her with her recovery, she knew from her own professional experience that the exercises which she would need to do, to achieve the aims she had for her physical recovery, would take an enormous amount of time. Although the physiotherapists would focus on the normal practice of keeping the limbs mobile, exercising and massaging them, Sheila knew that she would have to work for many hours on her own if she hoped to achieve her ambition of returning to her normal lifestyle.

'I knew that the exercises would take an extremely long time to do in my weakened state – time that the physiotherapists did not have to sit and encourage me – so I would work at it on my own. I would stare at one of my limbs for nearly an hour, mentally willing my body to obey me and try to get the slightest flicker of movement. One day I had been working on my right hand, mentally directing what I wanted my body to do, willing my finger to move. Eventually I was rewarded with the slightest flicker of my fingers, and I knew then that this was the breakthrough I needed, and that from that point on I was going to improve.'

Polio sufferers are very susceptible to the cold, and so were discouraged from leaving hospital in the middle of winter. They were advised to either remain in hospital until the warmer months or to leave earlier and try to acclimatize to the winter. Sheila decided that she could continue her rehabilitation herself and left the hospital the following October, to return to her family home to continue her recuperation. She was walking with the aid of crutches and in a spinal support jacket, which was made of thick pink plastic having been moulded to her body, and which provided support from her shoulders down to her hips. She was to continue to walk on crutches for the following two years, but was determined to end the use of the uncomfortable spinal jacket as soon as she was able.

In May 1954, just over a year since she had first contracted polio, Sheila then returned to Bognor and was continuing to work hard to improve her strength and mobility. Around the same time, one of the consultants in Bognor had been sending some of his patients to a clinic in Badragaz in Switzerland which specialized in using hydrotherapy. His patients had met with great success there, and he was convinced that Sheila might also benefit from this relatively new treatment. Dr Ferres had a friend Dr Beutner – not a medical professional but a lawyer – who had had polio at the age of two, and who also lived in Badragaz. Dr Beutner kindly offered to look after Sheila during her stay, and was able to help by arranging a suitable hotel for her near the clinic.

As she has already explained, Sheila maintains that she has always had the most amazing luck in her life, and been the very happy recipient of many fortuitous events, and this was to prove her point.

'I travelled out to Switzerland on my own, on my crutches and in my spinal jacket, and booked into a small hotel in Badragaz near the clinic. It was arranged that the head of the clinic would visit me in my hotel to discuss my case, and that we would meet in the lounge of the hotel for tea. I was absolutely amazed to see Miss Pfister walk into the room – she was of course the young Swiss physiotherapist whom I had fought so hard for, to be my replacement at the clinic in Cape Town. When she saw me, she said

'Now I can do everything possible to help you.' That's the sort of luck I have!'

Sheila was determined to make the most of her opportunity to improve at this world class clinic. At six o'clock in the morning, Miss Pfister would arrive at Sheila's hotel and run through her exercises with her. After this, they would return to the clinic for her hydrotherapy sessions. This involved enormous 'butterfly' floats which were attached to the side of the pool. The patient would lie on the 'body' of the float with arms stretched out on the 'wings', and then be gently lowered into the water. Each patient would then try to exercise their limbs, whilst supported by the float in the water. These exercises were exhausting and although there was a short rest period after lunch, the afternoon was spent doing yet more exercises but this time out of the water, all designed to mobilise and strengthen the weakened limbs. Sheila's spinal support jacket was taken off during the day, much to her relief, so that she could complete her exercises, but then had to be put back on in the evenings. Even though, she knew it was a necessity, Sheila grew to hate the discomfort of wearing her support.

In her usual manner, Sheila decided to put her time in the clinic to good use, not only for herself, but again thinking of how she might use this experience to help her patients in the future. As well as Miss Pfister who was from Switzerland, the Badragaz clinic had four other physiotherapists, one each from Germany, France, Holland and Belgium.

'We decided that every night, they would all come to my room in the hotel, and we would take turns to pick a condition and watch the other five demonstrate how they would treat it. So I got every single physio to demonstrate what they would do with a particular back condition, in their own country. It was fascinating to exchange our ideas, and even as limited as I was, I still kept learning and taking every opportunity that came to me so that I returned to England with quite a knowledge of exercises from all the other countries, in addition to being much stronger myself.'

After a few weeks of intensive treatment in Badragaz, it was time for Sheila to return home to Bognor and it was at this point that she decided to cease to use her spinal support jacket. She did however find another use for it and, on the journey home, she filled it with contraband – such as liqueurs which were not easily obtainable in England at that time – from Dr Beutner for his friend Dr Ferres.

Sheila religiously continued with all her exercises and also used her imagination and initiative to make some adaptations to her environment to make her life more manageable – as she had always done for her patients. As she had lost a lot of strength in her core and torso, she was unable to sit securely in a car seat, which was a painful lesson for her:

> 'I was in a friend's car one day, and as we went round a corner, the door accidentally opened and I was unable to hold myself upright and simply fell through it and fractured my ribs. I decided then that I had to have my car specially adapted and always drive myself. I had a special bucket seat made and as, in those days, you could alter the seat belts in cars, I had one crossing over the front and another crossing over the back to hold me securely in place. Unfortunately today, it is illegal to alter the seat belts in cars which makes it very difficult for me because they simply do not hold me. In a normal car, if I'm driven by someone else, and the driver brakes, even quite gently, I am apt to fall forward and hit the windscreen.'

Before she had gone to Switzerland, Sheila had only known Dr Ferres in a professional capacity, so she was a little surprised, but very grateful when he offered to pick her up from the airport on her arrival home from Switzerland, in his new sports car.

One of Dr Ferres's patients was Donald Healey, founder of Austin Healey car manufacturers, and Dr Ferres had recently taken possession of the second Austin Healey to be manufactured – the first belonging to Donald Healey. Sheila takes up the story:

> 'On the way, he decided that we would stop and have a meal in one of the pubs. It was pretty dark when we

entered the pub and I wasn't particularly secure on my feet. Several people were dining and I had to somehow get to my seat whilst threading between all these tables of diners. As I was looking down at where I was putting my feet and trying to be particularly careful, I didn't notice that there were decorative mugs attached to the beams in the pub, and that they were hanging fairly low. Being on the tall side – I was 5ft 11ins at the time – I walked into one of these mugs without seeing it and took it off its hook. It careered down into the soup of the person dining at the table beneath, and I had to apologise profusely to them. Fortunately Gordon and I were able to laugh about it and I felt then that we were going to become good friends.

Part of my rehabilitation, was to try to manage a short walk every day down to the sea and back. As I was passing Gordon's house on crutches every day, he arranged with his secretary and his daily help, that if they saw me going by, and saw that I was struggling to get down to the sea and back again, they were to invite me in and give me a cup of coffee, which they did from time to time. Gordon and I began to spend more and more time together and one of our favourite pastimes was to go for picnics in his car. I continued to improve physically, and about three years later, when I was able to walk again without support and had started my own practice, we were married in Bognor. It was the eighth of October 1958.

He was of course much older than me, sixty five years to my thirty five, but this didn't matter to us. As he was so fit and active for his age and I was a little slow for mine, we seemed to suit each other perfectly.

It was very important to me that I was able to walk and move about before I married, but my movements were still very, very limited, I could not walk far at all, and of course I was still very unstable in any car but my own specially adapted one. One of the first things Gordon gave me as a wedding present, was to have a special harness built and installed in his beloved sports car!'

Chapter 11

Sheila's husband, Dr Gordon Ferres was born in 1893 in the village of Echt near Banchory in Aberdeenshire, North East Scotland. He was a very energetic person, always busy even as a young boy, and achieved the highly regarded status at the time of becoming one of Lord Baden Powell's Chief Scouts, where he learnt many skills, amongst them Morse code. He attended Robert Gordon's School in Aberdeen, and never wanting to waste a minute, he used his journey time as he travelled to and from school to earn pocket money by sending Morse code messages up and down the line on behalf of the railway personnel. After leaving school at sixteen, he went on to study science at Aberdeen University.

In 1911, when Gordon was eighteen years old, he decided to set sail for Sumatra on a very small cargo ship, with the aim of working for one of the plantations out there. The journey took six weeks and throughout he kept a log of every port they visited and sent a postcard home from each one. His mother kept these for her whole life and Sheila was able to recently give this valuable collection to Ian Ferres, a descendant of Gordon's. Sheila recounts some of Gordon's stories of his experiences in Sumatra:

'On arrival, he was soon employed to oversee a rubber plantation, which was heavy going and pretty dangerous, especially for one of such a young age. One of the things he liked to do to get away from the stress of the plantation was to go big game hunting in the jungle, usually to help hunt a beast which was causing harm and damage by attacking local villages. These hunts often involved a long trek into the jungle, lasting weeks, to get to the right location. On one of these trips, 'G', as I called him, shot a tiger which then fell into a ditch which had been dug to prevent weeds getting into the plantation. G approached the ditch expecting the tiger to be dead, but it was in fact still very much alive, and grasped his leg with both of its front paws. G had one shot left in his gun, and as the tiger opened its jaws to seize him, G managed to jam the gun down the tiger's throat and pull the trigger. As the tiger died, its claws contracted and ripped G's leg open from top to bottom. In this state he then had to walk through the jungle for a whole week to reach the nearest inhabited village. During the trek the wounds became septic, and so when G finally arrived he then had to spend the next three months in hospital recovering.

On another occasion, whilst on a hunt with some friends G found himself being chased by a wounded elephant. G was carrying a rucksack which contained all the party's food and drink supplies, and in his haste to escape the elephant, he scrambled up a nearby tree, leaving the rucksack on the ground at the bottom. The elephant wrapped its trunk around the tree and shook it with all its might, forcing the tree to sway backwards and forwards in an effort to dislodge G. Fortunately G managed to hang on tight, and eventually the elephant realized that it was not going to be able to uproot the tree, and wandered off in search of new prey. Unfortunately for G and his friends, the elephant had trampled the rucksack and ruined all their rations of food and drink. They survived the long trek to their encampment by living off the coconuts that they could shoot down from the trees. Obviously they were starving when they did arrive at the encampment, but the only food they found was one tin of peaches and one tin of condensed milk. Naturally they consumed the whole lot immediately and were then violently sick. As a consequence of this, G would never allow peaches to either be served or even mentioned in his presence again!'

G left Sumatra in 1922 at the age of 29, following a rubber crisis, and decided to return to Britain to study medicine, where he attended King's College and Aberdeen University. Coincidentally one of his school friends, named Robert Douglas Lockhart, was now a Professor at the University and became G's university tutor, the two of them remaining firm friends for the rest of their lives.

G was man with a thirst for knowledge and capable of throwing enormous energy into anything he wished to achieve. In his travels abroad, he had found it of enormous benefit to be able to converse with people of various nationalities, and consequently he spoke six languages including Dutch, which he spoke with such accuracy that he was often mistaken for being Dutch. During his medical studies, G discovered a passion for golf and with his usual enthusiasm, he threw himself into mastering the sport, to the extent whereby in 1927 he won the Nairn Open Golf Championship followed in 1928 by success at the Spey Bay Open Championship. Sheila takes up the story:

'At Spey Bay, G had just come off the course when a gentleman spoke to him, 'When you have changed, I would like you to come and have a drink with me,' said this gentleman. G went off to change and as he did so, he suddenly seemed to develop a rather inflated idea of his own ability! He knew that he recognised the man who'd asked him to have a drink but couldn't place him and wondered whether he could possibly be a Scottish selector who was going to ask him to play for Scotland. As G sat down, he said, 'I'm awfully sorry, but although your face seems very familiar, I just cannot place you.' 'Ramsay MacDonald, Prime Minister,' the gentleman replied. 'I've come to present the prizes and I'm delighted to give the prize to somebody who doesn't even recognize me!' Obviously G must have seen his face on newspapers and suchlike, but this was 1928 when there were no televisions of course.'

On qualifying as a doctor, G moved to take up his practice in Bognor Regis in the South of England, firstly in the NHS as was required at the time and then privately. He had lived there for nearly thirty years in quite a small house, and when he and Sheila married they moved into a large house which had room for both of their practices. Sheila remembers their time there with great fondness:

> 'We had a wonderful social life in Bognor, and met all sorts of interesting people. My husband's patients were mostly residents of London, who had second homes on the South Coast which they visited at weekends. As a result, many of our friends were from the London area, and we were lucky to have friends such as Chesney Allen of Flanagan and Allen, and many respected business people including the Scottish philanthropist Sir Isaac Wolfson. G was also looking after the late King, when he was in Bognor and all the related families. Princess Alexandra and Prince Michael were regular patients because they spent their summer holidays in Bognor, and were kind enough to invite us to all the garden parties and so on, and so we had a very interesting life.'

Sheila and G only spent five years in Bognor after their marriage, as by this time G was seventy and due to retire. He was keen to return to his native Scotland to spend his time indulging in his favourite pastimes of fishing, shooting and golf. In the autumn of 1962 the two of them came to Banchory on holiday and to look for a potential home. They quickly found 'Greenferns', the house which is still Sheila's home over fifty years later. As there was some work which needed doing to the house, arrangements were made with local builders and gardeners that the jobs would be done over the winter months allowing Sheila and G to move in the following Spring. They returned to Bognor to make the necessary arrangements there for their move, but found that things moved very quickly indeed for them. As Sheila explains:

> 'Shortly after we returned to Bognor from our trip north, we found a doctor who had recently arrived from Nigeria, and who was keen to start a private practice in Britain. He immediately bought my husband's practice, along with our large house in Bognor, and kept all the furnishings

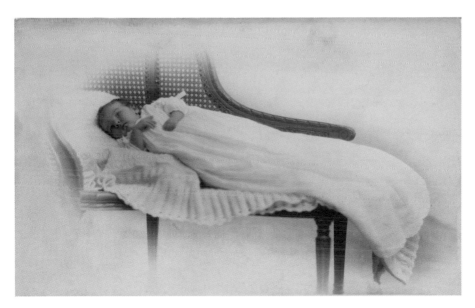

Above: Sheila aged three months, 1923.

Right: Pat aged 2½, Ailsa aged 1½, 1923.

Above: Sheila aged 1, 1924.

Right: Sheila aged 1,
Pat aged 3½, Ailsa aged 2.

Above: Nanny – Elsie Coates, with Pat, Ailsa and Sheila.

Right: Pat aged 6, Ailsa aged 5 and Sheila aged 4, 1928.

Sheila's mother, Elsie Bennett.

Sheila's father, Stephen Bennett.

Ailsa as an adult.

Sheila in Bulawayo, 1946.

General Smut's Memorial Service on Table Mountain, 1950.

Tennis in Rhodesia, Sheila on the left.

Giraffes in Bulawayo.

Sheila in G's Austin Healey, 1954.

Walton House, Bognor Regis.

Sheila walking on her hands, Walton House, 1960.

Sheila on arrival in Scotland, 1963.

Above: Greenferns, Banchory.

Right: G fishing at Woodend, Banchory.

Opposite page: G playing his fiddle.

Sheila in Zoute, Belgium, 1962.

Top: G on his 100th birthday.   *Above*: Sheila and G, on his 100th birthday.

Sheila presenting Professor Ralston of Aberdeen University with Sir James Paget's scissors.

Sheila in her uniform, in the garden at Greenferns.

Sheila on her 90th birthday.

Bennett House, Banchory.

Tough Going, exhibited Royal Academy.

Sheila at the opening of Bennett House, 2015.

Pail and Interesting

and furniture which were in it. We simply stepped out
of our old house, and he stepped in, and we came up
to our new life in Scotland and started again. Our house
in Banchory was small, with far fewer rooms so we didn't
need most of the things we'd had before – only space to
live in and a room for my physiotherapy practice.'

Sheila and G moved up to Banchory in March 1963, and stayed in the
Burnett Arms Hotel whilst the final work was finished on the house,
including the purchase of suitable furniture. Their housekeeper from
Bognor stayed with them from April to October to help them settle
into the house and then returned to her home. She was however one
of the many regular visitors Sheila and G always welcomed into their
house, and she returned every year for a holiday until she died.

Whilst Sheila and G were staying in the Burnett Arms, G met
an old friend of his, Angus Shaw, who was a great fiddler. Sheila
remembers:

'Gordon had played the fiddle in the students' orchestra
in 1900, over sixty years earlier, and thought that now he
had more time, he would start playing again. When patients
came he'd often be playing in the next room. One lady
tells me that she still misses it enormously because one
day, she was here on her birthday, and as she stepped
into the house, G played 'Happy Birthday to You'.

As soon as the house was furnished and we were
established, I decided that I was going to start another
practice because, by this time, along with the fiddle playing,
my husband had arranged shooting, fishing and golf and
was obviously going to be occupied from morning to night!
Although I have never fully returned to normal strength,
I knew I could still practise effectively. Fortunately my
husband knew a doctor from Torphins, near Banchory
and he spread the word that I was setting up again and
I waited for something to happen. It wasn't long before
the first patient arrived and from then on, it absolutely
escalated. I have never really been without work since.
I did domiciliary visits from Braemar to Aberdeen, and

the bulk of my practice has always come from the various estates, both employees and owners – recommendation by word of mouth has meant that I believe I have been to every estate in the district. Nowadays of course, I am treating grandchildren and great grandchildren of my original patients.'

Although her weakened physical state prevented Sheila from indulging her love of tennis and other sport, she did try to remain as physically fit as she was able by doing other activities such as walking on her hands and she did still cycle huge distances when travelling around both this country and abroad. As she explains:

'Cycling has always been a large part of my life. I've been twenty three thousand miles on my bicycle. I have a cyclometer on the bike which registers the mileage, and it is the same bicycle I was given when I was twelve years old. It cost seven pounds, a Raleigh, and it's still working. A few years ago, I took it into Aberdeen to get a new seat and when I went to collect it, the staff were all intrigued by the old seat. Apparently the underneath of the saddle was made of cement and they had never seen this before. They all wanted it so they tossed a coin to choose who would take it home. You might think a concrete saddle would be extremely uncomfortable, but in fact it was very much more comfortable than the one they replaced it with, very definitely. In addition to my twenty three thousand miles at home, I used to hire a bike whenever G and I were on holiday in Belgium, so whilst he was playing golf I would cycle all around the countryside and sometimes into Holland to go to all the flower markets and have a wonderful time.'

Sheila and Gordon had taken a holiday in Belgium, shortly before they left Bognor, and had stayed at the Majestic Hotel in Zoute, which was owned by Mr Tavernier, the Belgium Golf Champion. This became an annual visit and involved G meeting up with a number of Dutch and Belgian friends to play golf. Many years previously G had been

invited to play golf with King Leopold of Belgium who had heard
of his victory at the Nairn Open Golf Championship. They played
almost every day for a fortnight and became great friends, and when
Sheila and G happened to be in Belgium some years later, on G's
eightieth birthday, King Leopold's son threw G a wonderful birthday
party, and presented him with a plaque to commemorate it, which
still hangs in Sheila's kitchen today.

Whilst in Belgium, Mr and Mrs Tavernier asked Sheila to meet
and examine Kiki, one of their close friends who was the wife of
Billy van der Elst, an immensely rich cigarette magnate. As Sheila
explains the situation:

'Kiki was aged only forty two, and had suffered a stroke
due to a medical error. An injection had been put into the
artery instead of the vein thereby causing a stroke. She
had five children and was completely paralysed. After a
long journey to their house in the country, I encouraged all
the family to go out into the garden, so that I could spend
some time with Kiki on her own. I needed to see exactly
what she could do, without the whole family looking on.
I soon decided that I might manage to help her, and it was
arranged that Kiki, Billy, their daughter and Kiki's nurse
would travel to Scotland to stay in a hotel for six weeks,
during which time I would treat Kiki daily – they would
then return to Belgium for six weeks, before making the
return trip to Banchory for another six weeks of treatment
and so on. This arrangement continued for a number of
years, and I am pleased to say that Kiki did improve and
was finally able to walk, using a walking stick, and lead a
more normal life. Billy van der Elst gave me two beautiful
silver birds which now sit on my dining room table as a
gesture of his gratitude.

Sadly on the occasion of Kiki's last visit to us, she
was taken desperately ill with a life threatening intestinal
condition, and we had to make the difficult decision of
whether to risk her flying home or to try to care for her
in Scotland. My husband and I decided in the end that
she should fly home, and she died there a short while later.

We stayed in contact with Billy, after Kiki's death
and he decided to come to my husband's one hundredth
birthday party in 1993, and we were so looking forward
to seeing him. However he rang the night before to tell
us that he would not be able to attend after all because he
had tried to fix something on the roof of his house and had
fallen off and broken an arm and a leg. A few weeks later,
he rang again to ask how the birthday had gone and then
said: 'I'm phoning to say goodbye to you because I'm not
going to live much longer. They've discovered that I have
cancer and I do not have much time, so I've rung up to
say goodbye."

Chapter 12

Sheila has now been practising for over seventy years, and remains the oldest registered physiotherapist in the UK. Naturally her method of working has developed over the years as her experience has increased until she now has a routine which each session follows. She maintains that one of the most important factors is the amount of time she is able to spend with a patient exploring their own situation and discussing and teaching them the exercises they need to do. From personal experience she understands the patience and determination with which both the patient and their physiotherapist must work in order to see positive results. Sheila's first task is to find out as much as possible about their condition in that first phone call to make the appointment, and she explains how she then proceeds:

'When they arrive and park their car, I observe how they get out of the car, how they walk into the house and through to the surgery and how they sit down. I can then take up to half an hour asking questions such as what they were doing when the injury was sustained, what position they were in, and the force they were using until I have got an exact mental picture of what damage they could have done. This collecting of information is very important because there may also be environmental factors at work. For instance not many people understand that the height of a desk may not suit them. School desks, office desks and the accompanying chairs are all made a uniform height regardless of the individual's length of legs or torso. Many people can avoid some of their discomfort by ensuring that their chair and desk, and these days the height of their computers, are not causing them to hunch over or reach too far.

Another example of work related problems, comes from the number of postmen and women I have treated over the years, with terribly painful back and neck conditions caused often by the way they jump in and out of their vans a hundred times a day. Once I am able to explain to them the correct way to get in and out of their vehicles, many of them have found their symptoms ease.

When the oil industry was first established in Aberdeen, the helicopters were flying backwards and forwards to the rigs all day, and after a while the pilots began to develop back problems. As I was treating a number of them, Aberdeen University asked me to make a study of the patients and their work environments and to then discuss my findings. It was imperative that the cause of the problems was ascertained, whether it was a design fault with the build of the helicopters, the seating or perhaps something else.

My findings pointed to the fact that the pilots wore harnesses which were spring loaded to hold them clamped down and secure in their seat. However the controls were in the roof of the helicopter, and they had to consequently overcome the spring resistance to get their arms up, and so I was able to ascertain that their pain was due to a form of repetitive strain injury. To begin with, each pilot was given a back cushion which belted around his body, and which kept him in a forward position so that he wasn't going any further back than was absolutely necessary. It was then his responsibility to take his personal cushion from one craft to the next. As they began to design and build new helicopters, one of the key jobs was to research exactly what the shape of the pilot's seat should be and consequently, when the seats were changed, the problem was eliminated. Hence the importance of considering the impact of the immediate environment on a patient's condition.

Having gathered as much information as I can from the patient, I then spend some time testing and examining them to see how they can move and perhaps how they can't, until I have assessed their condition and what applied anatomy they require to get back to normal. Having finished all these movements, I then massage the area if that is required, and then go on to teach them the exercises I need them to do. I try to spend as much time as possible with the patient, explaining the purpose of the exercises, and what the ultimate aim is, so that when they leave they are fully aware of their condition, why it has occurred, what they need to do to improve it and also what not to do between each appointment or until we next speak. I encourage all my patients to keep me updated by telephone or further visits so that I can understand further how they are getting on. This means, of course that I get a lot of phone calls in the evenings, with reports and questions, and it has now got to the point where some patients will ring up with a question which I answer over the telephone, and I never actually see them. As I am now treating the second and third generation of some of my patients, I can often get a phone call from one of their children who might perhaps be at university, and unable to see me immediately, whom I can help over the phone.

It is often very worrying for a patient who is in pain and unable to move properly and they can often research their condition and make some assumptions about how serious their condition might be. As I am able to spend time reassuring them, they usually go away feeling much happier and optimistic, and hopefully physically improved or encouraged that they are going to improve. My patients understand that through my lifetime of experience, I know what their body should be capable of doing and the physiology of their muscles and consequently they trust me to help them achieve the best possible outcome. A positive attitude is essential to achieve a full recovery, and I understand that sometimes, if you are in pain and exhausted, it is very difficult to maintain such an attitude and to imagine a time when you may be free of your condition. I have treated several marathon runners, who love their sport so much that the idea of an injury stopping them from running is extremely upsetting for them. The story I tell them is the one about the young hurdler I treated many years ago. John was the sixteen year old son of one of my patients, who was a keen hurdler, regularly taking part in championships at all levels. Unfortunately due to injury, he had had to have the cartilage in his knee removed and the surgeon had warned him that it would take many weeks for him to return to his normal strength. There was a very important championship taking place a week later, and the young boy was devastated when the surgeon told him that there was no way he would be strong enough to take part. On returning home, John's mother rang me, explained the situation and asked if there was any way he could take part in the championship. I told her that in order to get his knee strong enough, he would have to perform a certain exercise every two hours, day and night, for the full week. In addition he would have to come to me the day before the championship for me to assess the strength of his leg and whether he would be capable of participating. The young man agreed to the conditions and so I showed him what to do. For the full week, he set his alarm for every two hours, both day and night and exercised his leg and knee, and then he returned to see me the day before the championship. I was happy to be able to tell him, after I had assessed him, that he definitely had enough power to safely do the hurdling and he promised to let me know how he got on. The following day I got a phone call in the afternoon from John who said 'You were quite right. I did the hurdling and I won the competition.' More proof of the positive results to be achieved by determination and persistence.

Obviously in the early years, different doctors might have agreed or disagreed with my treatment, but I am fortunate now to be in the position where my reputation speaks for me and a great many patients are referred

to me by local doctors for my opinion on what is wrong
before they return to their doctor to report back my
findings. One of the reasons I continue to be so busy is
that I am regularly taking on new patients, starting at the
beginning with them, and then making quite sure that I
am carrying them through until I've got them as good as
I can. There are times though where I have to send them
back to their doctor with a reason for their condition and
a message as to why I can't treat them and what I suggest
is done next. Over the years the surgery have learnt that
if I send someone down, the situation may be very serious
and require immediate attention, which is of course of
great benefit to the patient. For example, there was a
very well known gentleman from Aberdeen who came
to see me. I watched him as he got out of his car, and
as he climbed the front door steps, I noticed that as he
climbed the third step, his pattern changed. During the
consultation, he explained that he had had pain in his leg
for months and had seen several physios who all insisted
that as long as he kept up his exercises, his condition would
improve, but of course it hadn't. I spent well over an hour
putting him through different exercises and a variety of
movements, and came to the conclusion that I could not
make a definitive diagnosis and I didn't believe there was
any treatment I could offer which would benefit him. I did
however think his condition was serious and insisted that
he went straight back to his doctor and ask to be referred
to the hospital. Fortunately the doctor knew me and
consequently sent the gentleman to hospital immediately.
By the afternoon of the same day, it had been diagnosed
that he had a cancerous tumour in his leg and the relevant
treatment commenced. He wrote to me after he was fully
recovered to thank me as they had found it just in time.

I always discuss a patient's condition with them in
detail. That transparency is very important, partly because
it fosters a relationship of trust, but mainly because it puts
the patient in control of their own recovery. There are,
of course, people who want to improve but who don't want

to put in the work. To these people I often tell the story
of the gentleman who was a gardener, who suffered with
an acute shoulder condition. When he first came to see me,
he could hardly move it, so I showed him a very specific
exercise which involved him bending over and dangling
his arm down, and then swinging it around both clockwise
and anticlockwise. I told him that he needed to do the
exercise as frequently as he possibly could in order to
get a good result.

He came back only one week later and his shoulder
was completely cured. 'What have you been doing all
week?' I asked him. 'You must have exercised continually
in order to make a full recovery so quickly.' He laughed and
explained 'I work for Anderson Rose Growers, and during
our planting season, a tractor moves up the field digging
a series of holes and then another tractor follows behind
where someone places a rose tree by each hole. My job is
to follow along, pick up the rose tree and place it in the
hole, stamp it in and then move on to the next one. Every
time I bent down to plant a rose, I was in the forward
leaning position so I did my shoulder exercise three times
for each rose.' When I asked him how many roses he had
planted that week, he said two thousand, so of course he
had done his exercise six thousand times and had cured
his shoulder condition. This was further proof to me
that excellent results could be achieved by patients who
persevered with their exercises.

Sometimes, of course, I get people who for one reason
or another, don't pay attention to what I have said. For
instance there was a gentleman from Aberdeen who,
on arrival, immediately informed me that he had seen
nine physiotherapists about the pain in his shoulder, all
of whom had treated him and none of whom had been
of any benefit. After the examination, I said 'I'm not
surprised they haven't helped because you don't have a
shoulder condition at all. You've got a problem with your
neck.' He proceeded to argue with me insisting that the
problem was in his shoulder, and it took me some time

to convince him to let me treat him as I saw fit, not as he did. Of course as I continued to treat him, the pain began to ease and he began to realise that I had been right. He rather begrudgingly said 'Just continue treating me.' I found out that he was attending a high level meeting the following morning chaired by someone I knew, so after the session I rang my acquaintance and asked him to ask the gentleman whether he was feeling any better so that I would know whether or not I was the tenth physio. My friend reported that the patient was feeling a lot better, so I had the satisfaction of knowing that my diagnosis had been correct.

There are of course many people who want the work done for them – these are the patients who return to me having done the exercises once or twice or have forgotten what to do because they haven't done them at all. To be successful, I need the patient to take some responsibility for their own recovery, and I try to give them the information and guidance they need to do so.'

Sheila has had 15 operations throughout her life including three joint replacements. Ten years ago she was admitted to hospital on Christmas Eve to undergo a knee replacement. Shortly after her operation, she was visited by Mr Scotland, the surgeon, who explained that due to the holidays they were very short staffed and asked her if she would be willing to treat the patients and give them physiotherapy. Naturally she was unable to get out of bed having just undergone her own operation, so she conveyed the exercises for each of the patients from her hospital bed. She organized different classes for patients of varying mobility, motivating them to do their exercises throughout the day by encouraging and reminding them – even holding competitions amongst the more able. The improvement in their conditions and indeed their spirits came to the attention of the Ward Sister of the men's ward and she soon came to see Sheila to ask for help with her own problem patient:

"I don't know if you can help.' she said to me, 'I have a gentleman who's also had his knee replaced, but he seems to have given up. He won't attempt to move it at all, and not only that but he's reporting the staff and causing all sorts of trouble. We don't know what to do.'

As I was able to move around by this time, I agreed to visit him and see if I could help. When I asked him how he was, he replied 'It's absolutely hopeless. I can't move, I can't do anything.' I explained who I was and said that I was willing to help, but I was very firm and told him, in no uncertain terms, that it was up to him whether or not he did the work I would set him. I also explained to him what would happen if he didn't do it! I showed him the exercises, and told him to do them as often as he could and that he would soon see the benefit. The following morning the surgeon arrived and said to me, 'I don't know what you've done with that gentleman but he has been exercising all night.' The patient and I were in fact discharged the same day, and he and his family thanked me for the wonderful result he had achieved. Even in my hospital bed, I was still working. It just seemed natural to do so.'

Shortly after Sheila started her practice in Banchory, she began to treat members of the Kent family who owned Drumnagesk Estate near Aboyne. They had two daughters and one son, and the younger daughter Diana led a very active outdoor life, horse riding, gardening and on one occasion building a swimming pool. Whilst she was in the process of building the pool, she accidentally fell into it and of course with no water to break her fall, she broke her arm. She was taken to hospital where she consequently had her arm put into plaster.

On returning home that night, Diana was frustrated that the plaster cast was going to hamper her work as she attempted to finish her swimming pool, so she soaked it in the bath and removed it. The following day, she continued to build her swimming pool, lifting the blocks and setting them in place. According to Sheila 'The pain must have been unreal.'

When the time came for her review at the hospital, the doctors naturally asked where the cast was. Diana explained that it was getting in the way of her work and that she had removed it herself. The doctors were of course horrified and sent her for an X-ray to ascertain exactly what damage she had done to her arm. When the results came back, the doctors reported that the break in her arm was fully healed and the bones had knitted perfectly. As Sheila explains:

'This may seem strange, but from a physiotherapist's point of view, the lifting and so forth would have caused a great deal of friction at the site of the fracture and that must have stimulated the production of bone cells. Maybe she was just lucky, but it did seem that we all had to think again and that perhaps bones need a little more friction than is currently believed in order to heal properly.'

Diana's experience was going to prove instrumental to Sheila in probably the most difficult case of her career – the horrific car crash which almost took her husband's life.

Chapter 13

In 1969, G was seventy six years old and was travelling with three of his friends to Grantown-on-Spey to play in a curling competition. Sheila waved them off in the afternoon, wishing them luck in their match, and then began to prepare the dinner for the guests she had coming that night. At 9 pm the telephone rang, and Sheila was told that there had been a horrendous car crash, in which G had been severely injured, and that he was on his way in an ambulance to Raigmore Hospital in Inverness. His three friends were waiting at the hotel, with only minor injuries. G's words, as they put him into the ambulance were, 'Ring Sheila – she'll know exactly what to do.' Sheila apologized to her guests, but told them that they all had to leave because she had to drive immediately up to Inverness.

'When I arrived at the hospital, I went straight in to see G. He was in a terrible state. One side of his face was black due to a broken cheek bone and a broken jaw. His leg had eleven fractures, a number of his ribs were broken, his hands were broken and of course he had many internal injuries. The prognosis was not good and the doctors prepared me for the fact that he might not live. I spent the night with him in the hospital and then the following day I booked into a hotel. I made a brief trip back to Banchory to make arrangements for my practice, the house and so on, as I knew I wouldn't be back for a while, but of course I didn't know how long. So I stayed in Inverness for about a fortnight, arriving at the hospital at 6 am each morning, staying there the whole day, returning to the hotel for a few hours of sleep, and then back to the hospital again.'

G slowly began to improve until he was out of immediate danger, and after some weeks, Sheila decided that she would try to get him back to Aberdeen Hospital, and nearer to home. She decided that the most efficient way for him to travel would be by train ambulance. The side of the carriage directly behind the driver was removed in order to get the stretcher in, and G was lain across three or four seats in the compartment. The proximity of the driver meant that he could talk to Sheila and G, and ascertain that all was well, and so G arrived in relative comfort at Aberdeen Royal Infirmary.

Even in the seriousness of the situation, there were some humorous moments as Sheila remembers:

'When the surgeon arrived for his first consultation, G's broken leg was in plaster, but the other was not. The doctor said 'I can't understand what all these scars are from the top to the bottom of your good leg.' 'I was mauled by a tiger,' said my husband. 'Those were caused by tiger's claws.' Of course the surgeon thought G was hallucinating, and G had to tell the whole story before he was believed. I think this may have been the first time anybody had attended Aberdeen Hospital having been mauled by a tiger.'

G remained in hospital for several weeks to recover somewhat from his injuries but Sheila knew from experience that he would benefit most from the constant help and attention that only she could give him. Consequently she set about converting their living room at home, installing a hospital bed, with pulleys over it which would enable her to move G when necessary. When G returned home from the hospital, he was virtually blind due to the severe damage to his face and jaw, and could hardly move himself at all. Over the next few months, Sheila was his sole carer, having to look after him continuously – the accident had taken place in the November, but it would be the following April before Sheila would get a full night's sleep.

Obviously G had been a very active man, enjoying his sport and the outdoors and the most frustrating injuries were to his leg. There were eleven breaks down the whole leg and the instructions from the surgeon as he discharged G, were that on no account was he to put any weight on the leg at all. He was told to use crutches and 'Under no circumstances do you put your foot on the floor. No weight bearing,' When they had returned home, Sheila and G discussed the consultant's instructions. Sheila had remembered Diana Kent and her swimming pool, and voiced her opinion:

"I find it difficult to agree with that,' I said, 'because with eleven breaks and so many pieces of bone to heal, you're not going to get one complete line. It's all surely going to be arthritic too. I would have thought the best idea was to stand on it straight away – it will never unite with a smooth joint surface unless it has some compression.' G replied that he would do anything I suggested was best for his recovery. He put his trust in me completely.

I immediately got him standing on the leg which was in plaster, steadying himself with the crutches. Every exercise I suggested, he followed and over a period of time he began to be able to take his first steps unaided since the accident.

I measured the distance from the chair he sat in, through the house to the back door, and calculated that multiplied by one hundred and thirty two, it made half a mile. 'Once you've walked that distance one hundred and thirty two times without stopping, I'll know then that I can accompany you down to the Golf Club where you can sit and rest.' As with all my patients, I gave him a specific aim and the exercises to achieve it, and the day came when we were able to walk together down the Club, have a rest and then walk home again. After that, I would take him to a chosen area, but each time the aim would be that we had to walk a little beyond it, a little further every day.

Some months later, the day came when we were to return to the hospital for G's review. The doctor was of course concerned that G would be unable to stand when the plaster was removed, presumably because he hadn't been weight bearing for all these months, and insisted he take care as he didn't believe the leg would hold up.

When they took the plaster off, G stood up and walked out of the department and back. 'How on earth did you do that?' they asked. So we told them.

I knew that, to achieve the best recovery possible, G would need to believe that he would be able to take up his interests again, particularly golf. I devised a way to build a golf range in the garage, where he could practise. My idea was that this would give him back some of his independence – it would be something he would enjoy which would also strengthen his muscles. I took a large sheet and sewed it up the sides to form a large pocket at the bottom, and then hung the sheet against the wall in the garage. As G hit the balls against the wall, they would drop into the pocket of the sheet, and he would be able to take them out and repeat the action. Next came the putting green. I took a length of artificial grass, and cut a hole at either end. When he had finished hitting the balls against the wall, I would roll it out and he would practise his putting. His golfing exercises were enjoyable for him, and he also worked very hard at all the other exercises I devised for him, and consequently he finished up with the most superb result. Eventually he walked, played golf, drove his car, played his fiddle and did everything else he loved to do and he lived for another twenty four years.'

Chapter 14

Sheila has enjoyed warm and long lasting friendships with many of her patients and their extended families, none more so than the late Lord and Lady Cowdray of Dunecht. Lord Cowdray lost his left arm in the Second World War, but was a determined man who would not allow his disability to hold him back from participating in his favourite sports. By learning to do everything with his right arm, he was able to continue to fish and shoot, and was a highly regarded polo player. The first time he asked Sheila for help, was because he felt that he was losing the strength in his right arm and consequently was unable to hold his gun properly. It was arranged that he would visit Sheila early the next morning, bringing his guns with him, to demonstrate how he managed to shoot with one arm. Sheila takes up the story:

'At the time, there was a very small hut just above my gate, which was used by the local barber whose name was Charlie. Charlie had been there for many years, and as I had just started my practice, he was intrigued by all the folk coming and going. That morning Lord Cowdray arrived in his Range Rover and parked in front of my house. At that moment Charlie was walking past the gates and as soon as he saw the car, he stood behind the bushes to watch what was going on. Lord Cowdray jumped out of the car, introduced himself and within seconds he had picked up one of his guns, aiming it into the distance, to demonstrate his technique to me. Unbeknownst to Lord Cowdray, the gun was pointed straight at Charlie hiding behind the

bushes, and of course Charlie fell to the ground thinking
he was going to be shot. As Lord Cowdray lowered his
gun to exchange it for his second, heavier one, Charlie ran
into his shop and peered out through the curtains to see
what was happening. I, of course, was completely distracted
by watching Charlie, who was quite naturally terrified.
Fortunately it was something, we all three were able
to laugh about later.

This was the beginning of at least ten years of treating
Lord Cowdray whenever he came to Scotland, and
occasionally his wife. He usually came to my surgery,
but sometimes I would visit him at Dunecht House which
was a real treat. It was a magnificent house, with frescoes
painted on the walls all the way to the top of the stairs.
As you entered, there was a full size solid silver working
bicycle owned by Lord Cowdray's mother, which of course
fascinated me because of my love of cycling.

Lord Cowdray was a remarkable man who showed me
how he was able to do everything with one arm, knowledge
which I was able to use to help other patients. His great love
was playing polo, and he rode his pony with an artificial
arm holding the reins so that he could use his right hand
to hold his mallet. In those days prosthetic limbs were not
as developed as they are today, and a real danger for Lord
Cowdray was that if he was accidentally dismounted, he
would be dragged along by his artificial arm still being
attached to the reins. For this reason, his ponies had to be
specially trained to come to a complete standstill as soon
as he left the saddle, and to remain perfectly still until he
was able to remount. I saw him fall off myself once, and
the pony came to such a sudden standstill that its back
legs almost came over the front. The way Lord Cowdray
overcame his disability was truly inspirational. All the polo
championships are held at Cowdray Park in England which
is now famous for the sport.

One day in 1995, I was sent a message from Cowdray
Park to say that Lord Cowdray was terminally ill, and had
asked if I would go down to England and spend a week

with him trying to help strengthen him. I left immediately but unfortunately by the time I arrived, he had been admitted to the King Edward VII Hospital in Midhurst, Kent and he died before I arrived. As he was a close friend of the Queen and the Duke of Edinburgh, they were informed immediately, and as soon as that had occurred, the news was released to the general public and flowers began arriving at Cowdray Park from all over the world. It was the most amazing sight as every single flower which arrived was white.

Lady Cowdray had built a house of her own called The Orchard, so when she was widowed, she moved out of Cowdray Park into her own residence. I went down each summer to holiday with her for about the next five years. We got on terribly well, and had a lot of fun together. On one occasion, I had arrived on a particularly hot day, when she had just had an ice making machine installed. She pressed the button to release some ice into our drinks, but unfortunately she did not know how to switch the machine off, and so it spat out ice cubes all over the floor, just where I was standing. We had to wait until the machine completely emptied itself, by which time I was completely surrounded. Another time we got stuck in the lift of her new house, because we didn't know how to open the doors!

I've always tried to see the humour in a situation even if it is after the initial shock or distress have passed. One of my patients was Nial O'Neill, who was the cousin of Terence O'Neill, the Prime Minister of Northern Ireland during the 1960's. When I first met Nial, he had multiple sclerosis, and lived in a flat in Keith Hall where I visited him. Sometime later he moved to a purpose built bungalow down the road which would accommodate his electric wheelchair and where I continued to treat him. As he was never normally left on his own, his wife took advantage of my presence to go shopping, and so we were alone in the house. As Nial's legs were paralysed, the only way he could stand was to hold on to two supports, and then when he let go, he would sit down quickly and heavily. As we had finished the exercises and he was still supporting himself on the two handles, I got into his wheelchair in order to operate the controls to ensure that it was directly behind him when he sat down. Unfortunately I went too far, and just lightly touched the back of his legs. His reflex reaction was of course to fall back to sit in his chair – straight into my lap! Of course I did not have the strength to lift him, and so we were stuck like this for what seemed like an interminable amount of time. We did not know when his wife would return, and soon my legs had gone to sleep as well under the extra weight. Fortunately after about twenty minutes, the gardener passed the window and we were able to call out to him to come and rescue us!'

Chapter 15

Sheila's introduction to the present Royal Family came about in a very roundabout way. One day she was asked to treat Mr John Paton who owned Grandholm Estate on Donside. They soon became friends, and Sheila was to visit him weekly for the next sixteen years. As Sheila's weekly appointment coincided with lunchtime, they would often eat together, sometimes joined by other guests of Mr Paton. Part of the estate consisted of a number of cottages which were rented out and many of the guests were pilots operating in and out of Aberdeen Airport at Dyce. Late one night, Sheila was rung from the Grandholm Estate to ask if she would attend immediately to one of the pilots. Obviously she wanted to know the nature of the emergency so late at night, and so it was explained to her that the pilot she was being asked to see, was Captain Fielding, the Captain of the Queen's Flight. Apparently he had just brought the Queen to Balmoral a few days previously, and had since developed lumbago and was now barely able to move. The urgency was that he had just been contacted by Buckingham Palace, and the Queen had to return immediately to London the following morning. Sheila went straight over that night and after some hours, she was able to get Captain Fielding mobile enough to fly the following morning. This was the first time Sheila had treated anyone connected to the Royal Family, but as she explains it wasn't the last:

'In 1978, I received a phone call from Balmoral to ask if I would accept a Royal appointment. Of course I agreed that I would, and was then invited to Balmoral to be interviewed. Shortly after that, I was asked to treat

Princess Margaret, the late Princess Royal who had seen
many physiotherapists about a recurring problem. Princess
Margaret was absolutely charming, but a little surprised
when I disagreed with some of the exercises she had been
given. I asked her if I could proceed with the treatment
in the way I thought would be best, and after a moment's
thought, she graciously agreed. A few weeks later, I had a
lovely letter from Clarence House, thanking me as she was
delighted because she felt so much better.

As a result I was appointed to the Royal Household
of Balmoral to treat all the family, staff and guests when
necessary, and also the staff from Birk Hall, the Queen
Mother's former residence, which I did for the next twenty
years. Sometimes I went to the estate and sometimes the
patients visited me here – it was a fascinating period of
my life, and I have kept all the notes of thanks and various
letters they wrote to me.'

Obviously Balmoral and Birk Hall are just two of the many estates
Sheila has had cause to visit during her professional life. It has been
well documented that all the carpets at Balmoral are White Stewart,
which make navigating around such a huge mansion, very difficult.
As Sheila remembers:

'When there is never a change of carpet, you get to a
junction and think 'Where do I go?' Getting about is easier
said than done in some of those mansions.'

Just such a place was Glenkindie House, where Sheila would visit
Mrs Leith, the widow of the Honourable Jock Leith.

'My first visit to Glenkindie House took my breath away.
The entrance hall was sunken, with a polished grand piano
in the centre of it, surrounded by huge flower arrangements
of fuschia plants from the green house, and then a great
elegant staircase leading to the upper floor. Mrs Leith
was a tiny lady with a deep and abiding passion for swans
which were depicted on everything from the towels to the

bedheads. She also had an interesting solution to people getting lost in her enormous home. As she used to host many fishing and shooting parties, often for foreign visitors, people would be coming and going at all times of the day and night, so she devised a system which would prevent the need for her to keep getting up to show everyone where to go.

I arrived on this terrible snowy afternoon in the middle of winter, and as I approached the front door, I saw that there were two saucers on the floor each containing a piece of paper. The first was ordering fish for the cat, but the second was addressed to me and said 'Follow the white arrows'. I opened the door, entered the hallway and then noticed a series of white paper arrows on the floor, which lead me through the whole of the house until I reached the room where Mrs Leith was sitting. When I left, Mrs Leith told me how each guest had their own colour of arrow to follow to show them to their quarters but that everyone followed the blue arrows to get out of the building. An ingenious idea, I thought, which saved her a lot of work.

It was a system which may have come in handy at Breda House, another enormous mansion on Donside. I was asked to go there to treat the grandmother of the house, Mrs Lydall who had been in a car accident and suffered breaks both above and below the knees in both her legs. It was another dark wintry night in November when I drove over to Donside, and the only light came from the moon as I knocked on the door. Nobody answered and so I walked in, calling as I did so. The only thing I could see was the moonlight shining on to a staircase straight ahead of me, so I started to climb it. I climbed and climbed, and suddenly realized that I was going up into the turret of the house. I knew that could not be right, and so I began to descend back down, taking great care because of the lack of light. As I came down, I stopped to listen to a noise, which I was able to identify as horse's hooves and I began to wonder if the place was haunted. When I got back down to the first floor, I looked around and noticed a corridor with a light shining out from underneath a door at the far end of it. I went along to the door, knocked and was directed to come in. I had finally found Mrs Lyall, and after introducing myself, my first question was 'Would it be possible that I heard horses' hooves as I was going up the staircase?' 'Oh yes,' she replied. 'That will be my daughter exercising her horse. It has pneumonia and it's so cold outside, she must have brought it in.' Presumably this was not an unusual occurrence because 'Granny' as she was known was completely unphased to have a horse in the house. At that moment the bedroom door opened and in came her daughter – followed by the horse. The horse began coughing and the daughter explained about the pneumonia, and then promptly asked me if I could teach him any breathing exercises. Obviously we all laughed, and I said that I thought I would confine my efforts to human beings. I went on to look after three generations of that family, and each visit was full of fun.

Sometimes it can be very useful for me to have contact with the immediate families of some of my patients as I often glean little bits of information which the patient has either forgotten or chosen not to tell me. One day I was contacted by Major Smiley of Castle Fraser, whose wife was a cousin of Lord Cowdray, to have an appointment. Before his appointment his family informed me that his chest condition was worsening, and if he continued to smoke, his life was going to end shortly. At the end of his treatment, Major Smiley asked if he could have another appointment for the following week. 'Next week?' I said 'I'm not so sure that I could give you an appointment for next week.' When he asked me why, I explained 'I'm not making you an appointment for next week, because if you continue to smoke, there is a strong likelihood that you won't be here to attend it.' Apparently, he never smoked another cigarette since the moment he left my house that day, until he died four years later. His family were always grateful, convinced that he had the extra four years due to me.

Of course, over the four years I often treated Major
Smiley, and one Christmas, whilst I was visiting, he
asked me to accompany him into the garage as he had
a Christmas present for me. It was a beautiful, stationary
exercise bike which he thought I may be able to use.
I thanked him very much and took it straight home as it
couldn't have come at a more opportune moment. At that
time, my husband had had pneumonia and was struggling
to regain his fitness. G used the bike every day and soon
made the most amazing recovery. It was a wonderful
outcome all round.'

Sheila maintains that over the years, she has been surprised many
times when answering her phone as to who may be on the other end
of it and what they might need from her:

'Late one evening, I received a telephone call from a call
box. The voice on the other end had a very strong accent
and I was only just able to make out what he was saying.
'I be German visitor,' he said. 'Come Crathes by bus. Injure
my neck. Doctor say I put my neck out. You put it in.
Understand.' I gave him my earliest available appointment
which was the following evening at half past seven. I was
just telling him where to come when the money on his
payphone ran out, so I'd no idea whether or not he was
going to arrive. He did arrive however – along with a bus
full of German visitors, because he was the driver! He was
a very likeable person and fortunately I was able to help
him sufficiently so that he could continue with the bus tour.'

On another occasion, Sheila answered her telephone to a gentleman
who was calling from a telephone box in Dinnet. He explained that
he and his father were staying in a house on Loch Kinord, and that his
father was in terrible pain from an acute back condition, and asked if
he could bring him to see Sheila. Sheila, naturally, agreed and when
they arrived, she was surprised to see that the elder gentleman bore
a strong resemblance to Santa Claus, with a long white beard and a
mop of unruly white hair. G entertained the son in the garden whilst

Sheila treated the father in her surgery. During their conversation, the father told Sheila that they normally stayed at Balmoral as he was the Queen's shoemaker, and had made all her country shoes, riding boots and such for 'years and years'. At the time Sheila had been having great difficulty getting good leather slippers for G, and so asked this distinguished gentleman if he would be able to make some slippers for G. He replied that of course he would, and in turn asked Sheila if ninety pounds would be an acceptable price for the pair. When Sheila agreed, he then suggested that they swap the slippers for the treatment. Sheila protested that she had never charged anyone ninety pounds for a treatment, but he was insistent, and left with G's old pair of slippers to refurbish.

'When the two gentlemen had left, I said to G, 'Do you know who you were talking to?' to which he replied 'No idea'. I told him that he had been talking to the son of Eric Lobb, who lived in St. James in London and whose family have been shoemakers to the Royal family since 1600. He was most surprised when I told him that Eric had left with his old slippers.

A few days later the doorbell rang and the postman stood on the doorstep with the most beautifully adorned parcel. It was a shoe box with photographs and pictures of all the Monarchs around the side and on the top of it was the Royal Crest. When I opened the box, there was a beautiful shoe horn and slippers for my husband, lined with velvet with the Royal Crest embroidered on the inside. There was a note which read 'You said your husband had two pairs of slippers. If these are a good fit, send down the second pair – they are included in the swap.' I kept in contact with Eric for many years until he died. We exchanged letters each year, and one time I asked him what the normal charge was for a pair of shoes. He told me that one of his clients was a lady who had spent her entire life in a wheelchair, who ordered two new pairs of shoes each year, each of which cost her two thousand pounds. I considered that ninety pounds for a pair of slippers seemed extremely reasonable!'

Shortly after she had arrived in Banchory, Sheila was asked to attend Sir James Paget, who had suffered a stroke. He was the grandson of Sir James Paget who had discovered Paget's Disease of Bone in 1877, a chronic condition which often results in enlarged and misshapen bones causing immense pain to the sufferer and often requiring surgery and sometimes amputation. On meeting Sir James, Sheila remarked upon the fact that she had come across Paget's Disease quite a number of times when she had lived in the South. Sheila travelled to Ballater every Monday for seven years to treat Sir James, and on his death he bequeathed to Sheila his grandfather's bureau scissors and his stamp box as a thank you.

In 2000 Sheila received a telephone call from Professor Ralston of Aberdeen University requesting her help with the research he was doing into the back problems the helicopter pilots were suffering from, some of whom Sheila had of course already treated. He invited her to spend the day in the Orthopaedic Department and to have lunch with him to discuss the pilots' situation. On the day, Sheila arrived promptly at the University but was unfortunately kept waiting. When Professor Ralston arrived some time later however, he apologized profusely explaining that just that day, a team of international scientists led by him, had identified the gene responsible for Familial Expansile Osteolysis, a severe form of Paget's Disease. Sheila describes the moment:

> 'Professor Ralston asked me 'Do you know anything about Paget's disease? Have you seen patients with that condition?' Of course he was amazed when I told him that not only had I treated patients with the condition but that I had also treated Sir James Paget's grandson, and that I was now the possessor of Sir James Paget's bureau scissors. I told him there and then that, in honour of their breakthrough, I was going to donate the scissors to Aberdeen University.
>
> He was enormously excited and grateful and the brass encased scissors now sit in a beautiful mahogany case on the wall of the Bone Research Department in Aberdeen along with the history of how they came to be there. What a strange coincidence I should be at the University

on the day of their breakthrough in identifying the gene which causes Paget's disease. Quite unreal and also typical of my life, and something that would have pleased my husband immensely.'

Chapter 16

Sheila's husband, Gordon, remained very active throughout his retirement in Banchory, and continued to play his beloved golf for as long as he was able. His greatest achievement had been when he was seventy six years old and still managed to complete the Banchory Golf Club course in sixty seven – a feat unheard of at the club. Even on his ninetieth birthday the Club asked if he would challenge anyone to a round of golf and give the proceeds to charity. He did indeed play the match and naturally won. Eventually however he was unable to continue to play as Sheila explains:

'Unfortunately G had to stop golfing when he was ninety two years old because his sight let him down. During a round he found himself hitting white mushrooms in mistake of the golf balls. 'This time I have to stop,' he said 'when I am not hitting the ball but mushrooms instead!' As G's sight continued to deteriorate, he was eventually registered blind, and unbeknownst to me, the Blind Society used to come to visit him and record his life story. It was a complete surprise to me when they broadcast it on the radio on G's 100th birthday. We had a wonderful party to celebrate G's 100th birthday, and his dear friend Angus Shaw played him a piece of music which he had written especially for the occasion.

At the time my husband was the only medical graduate of Aberdeen University to reach one hundred years of age, and in his honour, the University decided that they would give him a presentation on 25th November 1993.

At the time G had been using a walking stick, but he was determined to be able to walk without it at his presentation. At the time he was staying at Annersley House, a private nursing home in Torphins, for a short respite and decided that he would use his time to practise walking without any assistance whatsoever, including going up and down stairs. Unfortunately during one of his practise sessions, he got to the top of the stairs, lost his balance and fell backwards, fracturing his ribs in the process. As soon as I arrived to be with him, he said to me, 'I've fractured my ribs and I'm definitely not fit. If I decide not to be treated, would you agree to allow me to die whilst I've still got so many of my faculties? I've had a wonderful life and I really do not want to be an invalid.'

I felt there was nothing I could do but agree to the wishes of this marvelous, inspirational man to whom I had had the honour of being married for thirty five years. G developed pneumonia, and when he was asked, he refused to take his medication and so slipped away in his sleep on 20th November 1993, aged one hundred years old.

The presentation at Aberdeen University was to be held five days later, and it was agreed by all concerned that I would attend in G's place. Throughout his life G had broken almost every bone in his body, but he had confounded many doctors with his remarkable ability to heal and so he had donated his body to Aberdeen University for medical research. I was aware that he was lying in the Anatomy Department, whilst I was in the main hall of the University reliving his life story and receiving his presentation. That was one of the most difficult things I have ever had to do.

As G had donated his body to Aberdeen University, after his death I also donated his 'pharmacopeia' to the Medical Department. A 'pharmacopeia' is a medical book relating to the dispensing of medicines, which are given to practising doctors as an encyclopedia of all the different medicines available. However G's pharmacopeia dated from the 1700's when doctors were making up their own medicines and using and developing their own practices and procedures. I know G would have approved of the University having such a unique and special tome.'

Chapter 17

By the time of G's death, Sheila had lost the majority of her family. Her mother had died in 1965, and her sister Pat the following year aged only forty seven, with her father passing in 1972. The late sixties and early seventies was a very difficult period for Sheila and her sister Ailsa as they lost so many of their close family in such a relatively short time. Their mother had become ill with a rare cancer of the gall bladder in the early sixties, and Ailsa returned to nurse their mother until she died in 1965. Ailsa remained in the family home, and Sheila visited her there on many occasions over the next 35 years.

In 1999 Sheila received a letter informing her that she had been awarded an MBE. In her own words:

'It was perhaps the greatest surprise I have ever had.
I was particularly delighted that it was not due to the fact that I had attended the Royal family, but for my services to physiotherapy including my work with the ex prisoners-of-war of the Japanese in 1944. I was sorry that G and the rest of my family were not there to share the moment with me but I was pleased that Ailsa was able to accompany me to the Palace to receive it.'

The following year Ailsa was found collapsed in the house and whilst she was in hospital, it was discovered that she had a cancerous tumour on one of her kidneys. Although after treatment, Ailsa regained some health, she was never able to return to the family home and instead settled into a private nursing home. Shortly afterwards she developed dementia and although she lived for another eight years, it was a period which would have a profound effect on Sheila as she watched her beloved elder sister battle the ravages of the disease.

'I visited Ailsa in England whenever I could. Dementia comes in various forms, but Ailsa had the vascular kind which meant that she would constantly be suffering from a series of mini strokes, each one of which would damage her brain a little more. She would be walking along seemingly fine and then would fall to the floor having suffered another stroke. Ailsa had always been a very gentle person, very kind and polite to all she knew, however as she got deeper and deeper into the dementia state, she became very aggressive. It was totally against her real nature, and near the end she was lashing out at the nurses. On one of my visits to see her in 2007, she was obviously in a very demented state. In a rarely lucid moment, I said to her 'Your life certainly doesn't give you a great deal of pleasure does it?' 'No,' she replied, 'You're right. It doesn't.' 'Well,' I said, 'if you think, by any chance, that you are trying to remain alive for my sake, then you must stop thinking like that. I know I will be the last surviving member of the family, but I shall be perfectly alright. I can manage on my own so you must feel free to do exactly what you wish. If you feel you just want to let yourself fade, you fade.' Two days later, the nurses went to get her supper and when they brought it back to her, she had gone. I believe it must have been a great relief for her. I do feel that she was comforted to have my assurance that I would be fine and felt that she could at last give up her own battle.'

As Ailsa had never married, she left her considerable personal estate to Sheila who decided that she would donate the money to charity. Sheila firstly donated two hundred and fifty thousand pounds to Aberdeen University for them to purchase a brain scanner. She felt this was a fitting tribute to the memory of her husband, and would also help further investigation of the causes and reasons behind dementia. As a result of this magnanimous donation, Sheila was visited by a number of personnel from the University who found her life story so fascinating that they have collated a large amount of information both about her personal life and her medical practices for storage in the University archives.

Sheila had obviously seen first hand how difficult it can be to care for someone with dementia. Due to this dreadful disease she saw her beloved sister behave in a hostile and violent manner totally at odds with her caring, gentle nature. On her many visits, Sheila knew how exhausting and exasperating it was trying to amuse Ailsa, but to also keep her safe and happy. For example she would remember how Ailsa would insist on going out into the garden and the time taken to get her dressed to do so, and then the minute they stepped out of the door, Ailsa would insist on returning to her room, only for the process to be repeated five minutes later.

Sheila would take a long time considering how to spend the remainder of Ailsa's estate in a manner which would be a fitting tribute to her sister, and which would also be a mark of Sheila's gratitude to the village of Banchory for the many happy years she has lived there.

Chapter 18

Since 1997, Sheila had combined her career as a physiotherapist, with a second career as a successful watercolourist. Although she had enjoyed art at school, Sheila had not done any painting since her schooldays although, as a student of physiotherapy, she was often complimented on the standard of her anatomical drawings. It was in 1997, when Sheila's friend, Elizabeth McIntyre, a retired physiotherapist, arrived for tea carrying a paint box, some pieces of art paper and two flowers. Elizabeth had been taking lessons for three years, and was keen to encourage Sheila to try it too. They had their tea in the summerhouse in the garden, and they each painted a picture of some heather, and another of a harebell. As was so often the case, Sheila was called away to a patient in the middle of their tea, and the summer house was left as it was.

As Sheila remembers:

'I never gave it any further thought – it was just a pleasant way to spend an afternoon. Days later, my gardener was having his snack and commented on the 'lovely paintings in the summer house'. Out of curiosity, I went back and had a look at them, and was pleasantly surprised. The Banchory Art Exhibition was to be held in six weeks at the Guide Hut, and encouraged by my friends I decided that I might as well submit a picture. I painted a country scene of a thatched cottage with hollyhocks growing up the wall, with a church in the distance, and country flowers everywhere. I entered the picture, it was selected and hung and on top of that it was the second one to sell.'

Over the next couple of years, Sheila continued to paint and was gratified at how popular her pictures became and the prices they could command. In keeping with her philosophy, she began to think of a way that she could use her art to benefit others, and so in 2000, she established her charity, 'CHART' – an amalgamation of Charity and Art, and since then every penny she has earned through her painting has been paid into CHART. CHART supports three charities, local to Banchory – the Glen Of Dee Hospital, the Forget-Me-Not Club, and the Thursday Club which meets the needs of sufferers of Multiple Sclerosis, Rheumatoid Arthritis and Parkinson's Disease. During the early days of the establishment of CHART, Sheila had a tremendous amount of help from someone who was a very close and dear friend. In her own words, Sheila explains:

'There are often personal gains in the work that I do, and I often meet the most remarkable people. For many years I treated a gentleman by the name of Gordon Gray of Craigmyle House, who suffered from Parkinson's Disease. During this time I became great friends with his wife Dorothy, and after Gordon died, Dorothy moved into a cottage on the Craigmyle Estate where I continued to visit her and attend her wonderful parties. Dorothy had been in banking all her life at a very senior level and so she kindly offered to keep the books for CHART. She took CHART under her wing, bought many pictures herself and encouraged her friends and family to do likewise and organized the design and sale of the CHART calendar which has become one of our most popular money earners. Unfortunately Dorothy developed cancer and died in 2003 – one of the saddest times of my life, and I have missed her more than I have missed anybody. The night before she died, Dorothy gave the name to one of my most popular paintings of flowers, 'You must name that Sweet Bouquet' she said. I knew then that she was weakening and so I visited again early the next morning, and was relieved to find her still conscious. As I sat with her I realized that she was failing. Her son was in the garden and so I fetched him in and the two of us were with her when she died.

I will be forever grateful to Dorothy for all her hard work
in establishing CHART and making it the success it is today,
the strong foundation which has enabled others to come
along afterwards and continue to increase the income and
thus benefit our local charities.'

Sheila paints in a small upstairs bedroom in her house, and calls
herself a 'minimalist painter' as the only things her 'studio' contains
are a small table, a glass of water, a paintbox and a piece of art
paper. Sheila began by painting from her imagination and using
still life arrangements, and then people would bring her their own
photographs often of their houses, which they would commission
Sheila to paint. Many of the pictures would be reproduced on to gift
cards of different sizes, prints both framed and unframed would be
sold and of course the revenue raised by the sale of the painting
itself. Sheila would never let an opportunity to raise more money
pass, and each year, regardless of the weather she could be found
sitting in a freezing cold railway carriage selling her cards at the
Annual Vintage Steam Rally in Crathes or taking a stall at various
art and craft fayres.

As her cards became more and more popular, many local shops
and establishments began to stock them. The Tor-na-Coille Hotel in
Banchory have always been great supporters of Sheila's work and
they currently have thirty of her paintings hanging on their walls,
and her cards for sale at the reception. Sheila has been commissioned
to paint many local hotels including the Potarch and each time the
hotel stock the cards to sell to their guests. The Finzean Farm Shop at
Finzean is owned and run by the Farquharson family, great personal
friends of Sheila, and another successful outlet for her cards, as is the
long established McEwan Gallery on Royal Deeside. One of Sheila's
most successful products is her yearly calendar, with each month
marked with one of her pictures completed in the year before. She
now sells about four hundred calendars a year, and they are sent all
over the world. Sheila has always been hugely appreciative of all the
help she receives with CHART, and one of those who has been there
since the early days is Mary Greig. Mary began by helping Sheila to
pack the cards of which she has done many thousands, but she then
decided that she wanted to make her own contribution to the charity

and so now she hand embroiders cards, gift tags, book marks etc. all of which are sold exclusively for CHART.

In 2005 Sheila found that she was two pictures short for the calendar that would need to go to print later in the year. Coincidentally a new patient contacted Sheila, George Booth who explained that he was a retired police inspector who was pursuing his lifelong enjoyment of photography. He had injured his shoulder when he had fallen whilst taking photographs and had come to Sheila for treatment. During the conversation Sheila asked George if he might by any chance have two local scenes which he would donate to her for the calendar. George readily agreed and has gone on to become Sheila's official photographer.

As Sheila observes:

'George takes the most beautiful photographs and many of the paintings that I have done were commissioned from one of George's photographs. George travels all over the area to the different estates where the owners will ask him to take specific views or photos and then I paint them. The paintings are sold before I even start painting – all thanks to George. George has also taken some marvelous wildlife pictures of animals such as herons or baby swallows, which I have again painted and have proved enormously popular as cards. As my sight is not as good as it once was, George prints off his photographs to reproduce every little detail.'

Sheila's sight around this time was in fact becoming very poor. She had developed cataracts over both eyes and for some years she was only able to focus within a narrow band down the middle of the field of vision in each eye. She often explains that this is why there is such fine detail on her pictures.

'As I could not see a picture in its entirety I would paint each picture strip by strip as I could see it. I had to make sure that the detail was exact as otherwise, of course, the picture would not fit together. Sometimes I would turn the photograph and the picture I was working on upside down and continue to paint from that angle.'

Some years later Sheila was able to have operations on both eyes to remove the cateracts and it was only then that she was able to see some of the pictures she had painted in their entirety.

In August 2013, Sheila received a telephone call from a lady in London named Mrs Starling, whose son had just recently been married on the Potarch Bridge, just outside Banchory. Whilst she and her husband were in the Potarch Hotel, they had purchased a number of cards showing Sheila's painting of the Bridge, and having explained that they were visiting their house in Torphins the following week, they asked if they could visit Sheila to see whether or not she had any other paintings which they may like to purchase. It was an opportune time as Sheila had just had six of her paintings returned to her from an exhibition at Balmoral which were in turn waiting to go to another exhibition. Sheila remembers their visit with huge enjoyment:

> 'Mr and Mrs Starling stayed for two hours that first visit, during which time we chatted about many things including my art and inevitably my charity. Towards the end of the meeting Mr Starling asked if he could buy one of the prints, which pleased me enormously. I turned to Mrs Starling and asked if there was anything that she liked. There was a pause whilst she looked around the room, and then she said to me 'I know exactly what I would like. I would like to buy the whole lot.' In addition to those six, Mr and Mrs Starling also commissioned me to do another painting of the Potarch Bridge for their son and his new wife, and another scene of South Uist from one of George's photographs. The total came to fifteen hundred pounds, and of course meant that I had nothing left to put into the Ballater Exhibition which was happening the following weekend.'

With her usual dedication, Sheila began work immediately to try to replace the stock of paintings which had been sold and thought nothing more of the sale. Unbeknownst to Sheila, Mr and Mrs Starling had been so impressed by Sheila's work they decided to try to help raise some money themselves for CHART. They contacted the framer who worked for the Royal Academy of Art in London and asked if

he would make prints of two of Sheila's pictures and frame them –
one of them was the 'Love of the Earth' and the other was the print
of Potarch Bridge. Sheila gave Mrs Starling permission to act on her
behalf in her dealings with the Royal Academy and so Mrs Starling
put both of these prints in to the Royal Academy Summer Exhibition,
with an explanatory letter. Shortly afterwards Mrs Starling received
an email back from the Royal Academy which read:

> 'Thank you very much for your covering letter. The lady
> you refer to sounds very inspirational. We have taken
> the liberty of putting the painting of the bridge and your
> covering letter on the wall of the Academy Office. None
> of the judges will see this. It will have no bearing on the
> competition but we were very impressed. Thank you very
> much.'

Twelve thousand pictures were entered into the competition that
year, which was seven thousand more than was anticipated and
unfortunately neither of Sheila's pictures were chosen. However
prints were made of the two paintings and with the sale of these
and the original paintings, over two thousand pounds was raised to
benefit CHART.

Chapter 19

By 2013 CHART had generated an income of one hundred and sixty nine thousand pounds to be divided equally between the three charities, the Glen Of Dee Hospital, the Thursday Group and the Forget-Me-Not Club.

Agnes McKenzie, Chairwoman of the Friends of Glen Of Dee Hospital, describes Sheila as a 'remarkable lady' who has donated over fifty thousand pounds to the Glen Of Dee. Sheila was keen that her donations would be used to purchase physiotherapy equipment which would be of benefit to the patients and to date they have been able to purchase special hoists, upgrade their ECG machine and provide specialist chairs. According to Agnes, 'The NHS would not have been able to give us these pieces of equipment, but thanks to Sheila, our wards are well equipped.'

Jean Wood is the Chairwoman of the Thursday Group (Banchory) for those suffering from Multiple Sclerosis, Parkinson's Disease and Rheumatoid Arthritis. It was in 2000 when Sheila was introduced to the group and decided to make it one of the beneficiaries of her new charity. Although the Thursday Group do have some other sources of funding, Jean describes Sheila as their 'Fairy Godmother' without whom Jean is sure that the group would not be able to function. Sheila is their Honorary President and remains very interested in the group and all the individual members.

The third charity to benefit from CHART is, of course, the Forget-Me-Not Club which had been founded in 1999 in Banchory by Heather Morrison. This unique charity was set up to help not only those who suffer from the different forms of dementia, but also to give support to their carers.

Sheila was aware that, although there were a number of different clinics all operating at different times of the week and dotted around various outlying villages, patients and their carers would benefit enormously from a safe and consistent environment in the form of a daycare centre. For some time, Sheila had been considering how she could repay the community of Banchory for the many happy years she had lived there, and she decided to put the remainder of Ailsa's inheritance from the Bennett family estate towards the purchase of a property in Banchory which could be converted to provide a purpose built centre for dementia sufferers. In 2013 Sheila was able to donate a further fifty thousand pounds from CHART, which when combined with the original three hundred thousand from Ailsa's estate, meant that a suitable building could be sought.

After a long and sometimes frustrating search, a house was purchased on behalf of the Forget-Me-Not Club, on Raemoir Road in Banchory. However it had taken all of the money raised to purchase the building, and there was still a lot of very expensive renovation and conversion work which would need to be financed. At around this time, Sheila was contacted by the estate of the Robertson sisters. They were three unmarried sisters who had formed a Trust and each year the Trust made a donation to a local charity. The Forget-Me-Not centre satisfied a number of conditions to confirm that it was a suitably deserving cause, and consequently fifty thousand pounds was added to the building fund. It was a very exciting time for Sheila and the other Forget-Me-Not supporters as the building work commenced the day after the Robertson sisters' donation was received. On 7th March 2015, Sheila officially opened the centre, named Bennett House in honour of Sheila and her family.

The purpose built centre has been designed with the help of some of the leading doctors in the field of dementia, who have advised on the layout, the furnishings, the floorings, and the furniture – all of which can have a significant effect upon dementia sufferers. It is a unique centre in Scotland where dementia sufferers and their carers can go, not only for respite daycare, but also for the most up to date advice and information about the condition. Naturally, as a charity, Bennett House requires constant funding in order to be able to continue to offer its services, and its many supporters are constantly fundraising from large charity events through to the coffee mornings held each Saturday at the centre and of course Sheila continues to make a significant contribution through her and her supporters' unstinting work to raise money for CHART.

Chapter 20

At the age of ninety three, Sheila is still working full time in her physiotherapy practice and also spends most of her spare time either painting, or continuing to raise money for CHART. By nature and also necessity she has always been very organized and methodical and admits to enjoying a routine to her day. Many people ask her how she continues to manage to have such an active life, and as she has already explained she feels it is the philosophy her parents encouraged in her, to always think of others, which is responsible for giving her the strength to go on despite her own health problems. Sheila explains how she spends a typical day:

> 'I usually spontaneously wake up just before 5 am,
> but if I wake any earlier, I will still get up as once I am
> awake I cannot go back to sleep. I usually make a cup
> of tea, bring it back to bed and then contemplate the day,
> what I am going to be doing, what I need to do and so on.
> I have breakfast at about twenty past five, usually a hearty
> breakfast as my appetite is still as strong as ever and then
> I will get dressed. As I have become less agile, it can take
> me some time to get dressed, but I then return downstairs
> and go into my surgery to check my diary for the day.
> The telephone will start ringing at around 7 am because
> many of my patients know that I get up early. My daily,
> who helps me with housework, arrives at a quarter past
> seven and she normally finds me at my desk sorting
> through the day's mail and dealing with anything which
> has arisen.

My next task is to deal with the accounts. I have three lots of accounts – those for the practice, my personal accounts and also those for CHART. I complete the books every single day otherwise it would be impossible to keep up with it all without getting in a muddle. I have always had a fairly organised brain, which helps enormously, because there is so much to consider. Naturally I have an accountant who oversees the three accounts, but I need to do the daily accounts because I couldn't possibly remember everything between each of his visits. I write things down as soon as a patient has left or I have finished a phone call, as a way of decluttering my mind.

The first patient of the day will usually arrive at either 8 am or 9 am. Each appointment lasts about an hour, so as one patient leaves, another arrives. This continues on until lunchtime which is usually 12 noon or 1 pm, depending upon the morning appointments. After again a hearty lunch, patients continue to arrive from 2 pm on the hour for the rest of the afternoon. Sometimes I go through until half past eight, with the last patient arriving at half past seven, but often the phone rings throughout the evening as patients update me on their conditions or their latest test results or just want to book their next appointment. I don't usually have a day off. I do try to take a day at the weekend, but most of the shooters, fishers and sportsmen and women want to come on their days off, and of course a lot of accidents happen at weekends. I certainly work five and a half days or more every week.

Obviously in treating others, I also take my own advice, and I have slept on a solid board with a very thin mattress on it for sixty years. Due to the weakness in my torso caused by the polio I have to lie absolutely flat to maintain an even posture. At ninety three, I can feel that I am beginning to stoop somewhat but I believe I have managed to remain fairly upright until recently, which is of course essential if I am to continue to work. By continuing to work and to remain active, I am aware that as I am helping my patients, the constant activity helps me also.'

In May 2013, it was Sheila's ninetieth birthday and although she was naturally aware that many of her friends and supporters would wish to celebrate with her, she was overwhelmed by the many shows of appreciation. Mrs McHardy of Woodend Estate organized a magnificent luncheon party, with many of Sheila's friends and patients attending, and several estate owners and their families. It was a warm and friendly affair and in some cases there were four and five generations of different families, all of whom Sheila had treated. The culmination of the party was when Sheila was presented with a beautiful cake which was a complete replica of Bennett House, with the figure of an artist, complete with pallet and paintbrushes, in the garden.

The week continued with different parties and dinners every night of Sheila's birthday and then several over the following month – the outpouring of such good wishes seemed to catch Sheila with some surprise:

'I was completely overwhelmed by everyone's gratitude and generosity. I could never have imagined such a vast number of people had appreciated what I had done for them. I have spent my life trying to help everyone in whatever way I could – it just seemed the least that I could do. People seem to be far more grateful that I could ever have imagined possible and I am deeply touched and grateful for it in return.'

In lieu of gifts, Sheila's birthday guests contributed to the fund for Bennett House and another five thousand pounds was raised towards the purchase of the specialist furniture needed for the centre.

Although Sheila has had some of her own health problems in recent years she continues to try to overcome them, and focus on her work, her fundraising and her painting. The establishment of the Bennett Centre has been a tremendous driving force throughout the last decade for Sheila and now that it is open, she continues to find ways to contribute towards its running costs. As she says:

'I feel responsible for having started it, and for having contributed to it, and I am really very pleased to think that my latter years have benefitted the community, and I have been able to give back to them in the same way they have given to me. So I shall continue to enjoy life knowing what a success it has been and will continue to be, for the community.

I often wonder what I'd be like now if I hadn't had polio. Still climbing mountains probably. But I've loved it and I had my day to succeed. I was lucky. I'm still lucky. I still enjoy life, very much so, and every day something's going to happen and I am going to enjoy it. I've done so much in my life that it's not easy to put it all down on paper, but I hope I have included all the important parts and that they have been of some interest and use to other people.

For all this luck and pleasure, I have to thank my parents and the upbringing they gave me. We could have been thoroughly spoiled, only thinking of ourselves, but we were encouraged to be thankful for everything, and I continue to be immensely and most especially grateful to them both for the nature they gave me and the ability to enjoy life that I inherited from them.

Before I go to sleep at night, I lie in my bed and think about the day. Each night I wonder how I would answer my parents if they were here to ask me the question 'What have you done today for somebody else?' I consider what I have achieved and how I have helped someone else or maybe several people.

I like to have Radio Four playing quietly in the background as I sleep, and I often drift in and out of consciousness, listening to some of the pieces of music, particularly Chopin, that my parents would either play or sing for us on those precious Sunday afternoons so many years ago. My greatest regret is that none of my family were able to live long enough to see what I have achieved in the latter half of my life, but when I hear the music that my parents loved, I feel myself taken back to the family parlour, singing and laughing with my parents and my sisters, and I like to believe that they would have been proud of me.'